KEYS TO CHOOSING A
FINANCIAL SPECIALIST

Raymond J. Lipay, CPA, MBA

BARRON'S

Copyright ©1992 by Barron's Educational Series, Inc.

All inquiries should be addressed to:
Barron's Educational Series, Inc.
250 Wireless Boulevard
Hauppauge, New York 11788

Library of Congress Catalog Card No. 91-4905

International Standard Book No. 0-8120-4545-9

Library of Congress Cataloging-in-Publication Data

Lipay, Raymond J.
    Keys to choosing a financial specialist / Raymond J. Lipay.
      p.   cm—(Barron's business keys)
    Includes index.
    ISBN 0-8120-4545-9
    1.   Financial   planners.   2.   Accountants.   I.   Title
    II. Series.
    HG179.5.L57
    332.024—dc20   91-4905
                                              CIP

CONTENTS

INTRODUCTION

When professional investment services are needed, it is important to choose someone with the right expertise. When a car fails to operate, you bring it to an automobile mechanic. If there is an electrical wiring problem in your home, you call a licensed electrician. The same thinking applies to financial matters and it is important to know the steps to take that will help you choose the right financial specialist.

The four financial specialists that will be discussed in this book are: certified public accountants (CPAs), financial planners, money managers, and stockbrokers. There is often a misconception regarding the extent of services performed by these four financial specialists.

A certified public accountant (CPA) for example, is perceived as someone who prepares income-tax returns and keeps books of accounts. However, these functions are the "tip of the iceberg" when it comes to services CPAs provide.

Financial planners, money managers, and stockbrokers are often thought of as being pretty much the same. To a certain extent their functions are complementary, but each of these specialists provides distinct services.

The keys in this book provide invaluable information when considering which financial specialist is the right one for your specific individual or business financial goals and needs. For example, in order to distinguish among the four financial specialists, the specific services provided by each of these professionals are described. This information should also enable you to focus on deciding whether a CPA, financial planner, money manager, or stockbroker is best suited to helping you achieve your financial objectives.

This book also includes keys that cover the various factors to use in selecting the most qualified financial specialists, and some guidance on fees for these services.

1

Using criteria such as education, training, experience, and professionalism, each financial specialty is discussed. Guidelines for hiring and firing a financial specialist and tools for deciding whether they are handling the job in a competent and professional manner are also addressed. Monitoring the performance of your chosen CPA, financial planner, money manager, or stockbroker is also discussed.

Interview questionnaires are included as appendices; these can be used to screen the most qualified CPA, financial planner, money manager, and stockbroker. The questionnaires can serve as memory joggers when interviewing a prospective candidate.

By using these skills, you will be well equipped to make an intelligent and informed decision when choosing a financial specialist.

1

SERVICES PROVIDED BY CPAs

The technical knowledge, training, and experience of certified public accountants (CPAs) enables them to provide a variety of services in addition to the accounting, bookkeeping, and taxation services commonly associated with this profession. CPAs are also qualified to offer services relating to financial statements, advisory and consulting services, as well as financial planning.

Accounting Services. Accounting services provided by a CPA include bookkeeping tasks and the maintenance of accounting records: writing up books of original entry, preparing journal entries, reconciliation of bank accounts, and adjusting and closing books. CPAs often provide these services in conjunction with compiling financial statements.

Financial Statements. Financial statements are helpful when an individual is planning to start a small business or is running a business. Individuals involved with estate and retirement planning may also find financial statements helpful. These statements can be used to secure a bank loan, raise capital from potential investors, acquire another business, or sell all or a portion of its operations. The basic financial statements for a business include the following: a balance sheet, an income statement, a statement of cash flows, and accompanying notes.

Individuals and families may require personal financial statements when organizing and planning their financial affairs: obtaining credit, income-tax planning, estate and retirement planning, etc. Some individuals may also be concerned with public disclosure of their financial affairs—those involved in or seeking public office, for example.

Personal financial statements generally include a statement of financial condition and a statement of changes in net worth. An accurate set of financial statements allows a user of those statements, such as a banker, to understand how your financial affairs are organized. Properly prepared financial statements also demonstrate that you are able to maintain your financial records in a timely manner.

A CPA can provide any of three distinct services in ensuring the development of an accurate set of financial statements. These three services are: 1) audits, 2) reviews, and 3) compilations.

Audits. An audit is the highest level of service a CPA provides in relation to financial statements. Audits involve the study and evaluation of a company or individual's internal control structure. This includes the methods and procedures for ensuring the protection or safeguarding of assets, and the reliability of financial records. Based on a review of these controls, the CPA uses auditing procedures to test selective transactions as they pertain to cash, accounts receivable, accounts payable, and other accounts.

Generally, individuals have adequate control over safeguarding their assets, but do not have a formal system of recording transactions. An adequate system of internal control for an individual requires complete financial records so that a CPA can determine the nature and extent of any transactions—the purchase or sale of securities or property, for example. This information is especially important when preparing income-tax returns.

Reviews. During a review of financial statements, the CPA inquires about accounting policies, recordkeeping, and other matters, and also performs analytical procedures to identify any unusual trends in financial statements. Because of the limited nature of the work performed by a CPA during a review as compared to an audit—namely, inquiries and analytical procedures—a review is not designed to express an opinion on financial statements taken as a whole. A review is also not designed to assure that all significant matters normally disclosed in an audit will be brought to the CPA's attention.

Compilations. For a compilation, the CPA prepares financial information in a financial statement format based on client-supplied data.

Taxation Services. Preparing income-tax returns is only

one facet of taxation services that CPAs provide to individuals and small businesses. A CPA with tax expertise can also offer the following services:

Tax consulting—advice on minimizing estate and gift-tax burdens on transfers of ownership among family, design compensation and fringe-benefit plans, and guidance on the tax impact of financial settlements in relation to separation and divorce arrangements.

Tax compliance—reviewing tax returns, computing estimated tax payments for individuals and small businesses, assisting in preparing tax-accrual provisions for financial statement presentations.

Representation—assistance before tax authorities such as the Internal Revenue Service and state authorities during an examination.

Personal Financial Planning. CPAs can also develop formal financial plans for individuals and businesses. This type of service is discussed more fully in Keys 14 to 26.

If you have a small business, an audit may be required if:

- You are an absentee owner and company operations are carried out by others.
- You are trying to solidify a loan agreement with a bank or for a line of credit.
- A major supplier and/or customers request audited financial statements.
- You want to strengthen the company's financial credibility to a potential buyer or partner.

If you require financial statements for yourself or for your small business, in most instances a review or a compilation will suffice. This is usually the case when your banker knows you from prior dealings, as a result of a long-term relationship, or if outstanding company debt is low.

If you require a loan for individual needs or for family-owned business, a bank generally will be satisfied with reviewed or compiled financial statements.

For example, a policeman in the Midwest decides to retire after twenty years on the force and open a dry-cleaning store. He approaches his local bank for a small-business loan. The loan officer requests a compiled set of personal financial statements as a basis for granting the loan.

2

DIFFERENCES BETWEEN CPAs AND OTHER ACCOUNTANTS

In today's business environment, "accountant" is a generic term used to refer to bookkeepers, tax preparers, business managers, controllers, and financial consultants. Only a select group of accountants are CPAs.

In general, a CPA is someone who has demonstrated competence and skill as a licensed professional accountant by meeting certain statutory requirements of a state or territory. This includes all fifty states, the District of Columbia, Puerto Rico, the Virgin Islands, and Guam. These statutory requirements include: 1) meeting high educational standards, 2) passing a uniform exam, and 3) working in public accounting for a certain period of time.

Education of a CPA. Most states require a CPA candidate to have a bachelor's degree from an accredited college or university of which at least 150 hours must be courses in accounting, related business subjects, and liberal arts. A graduate degree is also becoming common among CPAs. For example, many colleges and universities offer a combination bachelor's and master's degree program in accounting that allows for at least two years of preprofessional preparation and three years of more advanced professional-level studies.

When someone becomes a CPA, the education process continues. To keep pace with the profession's expanding body of knowledge, most states require CPAs in public practice to take 120 hours of continuing professional education (CPE) over a three-year period. Failure to fulfill CPE requirements may result in revocation of a CPA certificate. For example, a CPA in North Dakota had his CPA certificate revoked by the North Dakota State Board of Public Accountancy because he failed to comply with the Board's CPE requirements. In most states, a CPA license is renewable every three years. A program for meeting a state's CPE requirements generally includes subjects relating to accounting, auditing, taxation, and management advisory services.

The education requirements for an accountant who aspires to be a CPA are more rigid and structured as compared to a non-CPA accountant. A high-school diploma is generally the only academic preparation necessary for a bookkeeper and a tax preparer. In some cases, some advanced training might be necessary, such as specific courses in a business school.

The CPA Examination. In order to become a CPA, an individual must pass the CPA examination, which is uniform throughout all states. The exam encompasses a two-and-a-half-day accounting achievement test that is designed to determine a CPA candidate's knowledge of accounting practice, auditing standards, accounting theory, and business law. The CPA exam is administered twice a year by the state boards of accountancy.

As technology increases the demands placed on the public accounting profession, testing methods are revised to ensure that prospective CPAs possess certain entry-level skills. For example, beginning in 1994, the CPA examination will be restructured to encompass the following sections:

1. Auditing.
2. Professional responsibilities and business law.
3. Accounting and reporting as related to taxation and managerial, government, and not-for-profit organizations.
4. Financial accounting and reporting as related to business enterprises.

Work Experience of CPAs. Most states require a CPA candidate to work as an accountant or auditor for a certain period of time (e.g., three years) in public accounting or as an auditor for the federal government. However, in some states a master's degree can be substituted for partial or complete fulfillment of the work-experience requirement. For most non-CPA accounting jobs, there are no specific work experience requirements.

3

METHODS OF FINDING
A CPA

After deciding on the *type* of CPA service or services you require, the next step is finding the right CPA. In most cases this should not pose a problem, since there are several thousand practicing CPAs in the United States and the number continues to increase.

The most common approach for finding a CPA is similar to searching for an attorney or a physician—through referrals and/or recommendations. Your attorney, banker, or insurance agent often works with CPAs. Other sources of referral may be contemporaries in your line of business or profession. Personal friends and neighbors are another basic source of referral for a CPA, especially when it relates to tax-return preparation.

The society of CPAs located within your home state is also a source of referral. Many of these organizations provide referral services through which potential clients can discuss particular needs and preferences for accounting and other CPA services. Potential clients are given the names of CPA firms that practice within their city or town. Initial consultations between the potential client and a particular CPA firm can be arranged by the state society. In most states, this type of referral service is free of charge and can be used until a suitable CPA is found.

Many CPA firms conduct seminars on specific business subjects and taxation areas. If these seminars cover a subject that relates to your specific need, the firm or individual CPA conducting the seminar should be considered.

Other sources for finding a CPA include your local Chamber of Commerce, Rotary Club, and other business organizations. Some educational groups, such as college or university alumni associations, also provide referrals.

Many CPAs advertise their services in newspapers and other publications. However, since published ads are often designed to make someone look good on paper, they should not be used as a final criterion.

Regardless of the method used to narrow the search for the right CPA, meetings with a prospective CPA followed by a request for references from the CPA's clients are essential. Meetings and references will also help you focus on the various factors to consider in choosing the right CPA, all of which are covered in the remaining keys of this section.

4

TECHNICAL COMPETENCE

The most important factor to consider in selecting a CPA is the technical competence of the CPA or accounting firm. Technical competence hinges upon three important items:

- Education.
- Training.
- Experience.

By investigating the extent of the CPA's technical competence, you can determine whether your individual and/or business needs can be fulfilled.

For example, if you own income-producing properties, your CPA should be familiar with all aspects of taxation relevant to real estate—such as allowable depreciation and passive losses—in order to afford you favorable tax advantages.

If you own and operate a business, the technical competence of your CPA should extend beyond bookkeeping services, financial-statement preparation, and preparing tax returns. Advice and business counseling in the following areas is critical: budget preparation, internal accounting controls, compliance with government regulations, cash management, long-range and strategic planning, capital planning, and raising capital for expansion purposes.

When it comes to raising capital, a CPA can serve as an important intermediary between a client and its bank.

For example, when a loan is needed, the most effective way to justify the loan is through a written loan proposal. This is especially important if you are starting your own business and you have no track record. A well-thought-out loan proposal prepared with the assistance of a CPA should present a small-business owner's case effectively. A CPA can help the owner document how the funds will be used and, more important, how and why the repayment plan will work.

Technical competence implies that the CPA is familiar with the nature of your company's business. Ideally, the CPA should have clients in the same industry. Based on this experience, the CPA should be well qualified to perform the services your company needs. Like doctors and lawyers who specialize in certain areas, a CPA may be a specialist in particular industries.

Industry experience is especially important in services related to financial statements, such as audits, reviews, and compilations. Certain companies have accounting and financial-statement disclosure requirements that are unique to the industries of which the companies are a part; construction, finance, and not-for-profit organizations are examples. For instance, if you need financial statements for estate-tax purposes, your CPA should be familiar with the special treatment and presentation style required for personal financial statements.

In determining a prospective CPA's technical competence within the area of your individual or business needs, find out if the firm has serviced similar clients, and ask if you might contact those clients as a reference check. Also, determine whether the CPA firm requires continuing professional education (CPE) in the areas relating to your needs (e.g., estate and tax planning or cash management). In this way, you can be the final judge on the technical competence of your CPA.

Never assume that a CPA is competent in all business and financial areas. In order to obtain new business, some CPAs have been known to "bite off more than they can chew." For example, one CPA was selected from a telephone directory to audit a publicly listed company. The CPA lacked the necessary experience to handle the SEC-related engagement. This resulted in the issuance by the audited company of financial statements that misrepresented the company's financial position. If the CPA had "hands on" experience in auditing publicly held companies, he might have detected the problem.

The moral of this story? Be certain that your CPA has the necessary technical competence by way of education and experience. An ethical, professional CPA will not undertake an assignment for which he or she is unsuited.

5

CHOOSING A TAX PREPARER

Throughout most of our lifetime, we have to file income-tax returns. We often require professional help in preparing those returns, because of the complicated and changing nature of tax laws.

The complexity of your income-tax return rather than the size of your income should be the determining factor in deciding whether you need the assistance of a CPA. For example, as the executor of a friend's estate, a businessman was astonished to find that in order to pay the estate taxes, he would have to sell a large portion of the estate's property, which would leave the heirs almost destitute. That experience prompted him to hire a CPA to arrange his personal estate to take advantage of benefits and exemptions to enhance his family's financial security.

If your income is limited to wages and interest income, and you do not itemize deductions, a local Internal Revenue Service (IRS) office can assist you in preparing a short form, 1040-A or 1040-EZ. You may be able to complete these forms yourself.

The assistance of a CPA should be sought whenever you have any one or more of the following:

- Various deductions that warrant itemizing.
- Interest and dividend income.
- Multiple stock transactions.
- Tax-shelter investments.
- Rental-income property.
- Dependent children.
- A pension distribution.
- Mortgage payments.
- A casualty loss or theft of property.

An unmarried schoolteacher whose only income was wages and interest income from two savings accounts always prepared her own short form 1040-A. When an elderly aunt died, the schoolteacher inherited shares of stocks and bonds. Since she was unsure how to treat the income generated from these securities, she sought the advice of her insurance agent, who recommended a CPA who worked with the agent on an estate-planning team.

If your total income from wages and other sources exceeds $50,000, or you own a business, a CPA should be considered for tax-return preparation to cover any questionable areas that might affect your return, such as business and home-office deductions.

For example, a retired engineer organized a small consulting service. After one year, he had a thriving business with a large tax burden. He called a CPA who organized the records, took advantage of certain tax provisions, and prepared an income-tax return that saved the engineer hundreds of dollars. Two years later, when the IRS audited his return, the engineer, accompanied by his CPA, was prepared to explain how all the figures evolved.

Look for a CPA who is familiar with current tax laws, IRS rules and regulations, and the latest rulings in tax-law cases.

For example, the founder of a small family-owned corporation was preparing to retire and decided to have a full review of his company's tax situation. He engaged a CPA, who discovered that the company had overlooked tax provisions that specifically benefited the company. Based on a thorough review by the CPA of the company's inventory-costing method and depreciation schedules, the company realized a tax savings of more than $1 million.

Determine whether the CPA will represent you before the IRS in the event your tax return becomes subject to an audit. Also, find out whether the CPA has any experience before the IRS Appellate Division, which is where you go to appeal your case if you and the examining IRS agent fail to come to an agreement with regard to your tax audit. If a CPA has this experience, he or she will probably not accept an examining IRS agent's first offer too readily.

Inquisitiveness on the part of a CPA is important in tax-related matters. For example, a CPA who questions any decreases in interest and dividend income from the prior year to the current year is probably looking below the surface of the numbers and considering the possibility of sales and securities that may result in taxable capital gains.

Look for a CPA who can provide you with continual tax-planning alternatives as well as with intelligent tax-return preparation.

For example, a director for a nonprofit agency was experiencing difficulty in supporting two children and making ends meet after a divorce. She turned to a CPA who showed her how to keep better track of charitable contributions, provided advice on child-care deductions, and urged her to cut nonessential spending in order to fund an individual retirement account (IRA).

If you are in the market for present and/or future tax-planning advice, avoid a local public accounting firm that maintains books for its clients on a year-round basis and prepares tax returns only during the regular income-tax season (i.e., January through April). Always avoid using a CPA who does any of the following:

- Quotes the Internal Revenue code throughout conversations. He or she is probably only trying to impress you.
- States that no client of his or her firm ever gets audited. In light of the many gray areas of the IRS Code, any such claim should be regarded with suspicion.
- Promises a refund, or a fee based on the percentage of any refund.

Consider having a planning session with a prospective CPA, especially if you require tax-planning services on an ongoing basis. A planning session should be scheduled sometime in October or November. The CPA should give you some idea as to your expected liability based on information you provide about income and deductions. (You will probably be charged for the tax-planning session.)

The cost of a planning session may be worthwhile, because the session affords you the opportunity to ask the CPA pertinent questions about your tax situation and about his or her experience and expertise in tax-related matters. The most important benefit of a tax-planning session is that it allows you to determine whether the CPA appears to be receptive to building an ongoing business relationship.

6

WORKING WITH
YOUR CPA FIRM

A cooperative CPA-client relationship is essential for the successful completion of any type of CPA-related service. When you engage a CPA for any service, try to make the engagement run as efficiently and smoothly as possible. This can be accomplished in several ways.

When you meet with your CPA for the purpose of engaging services, such as the preparation of personal financial statements and/or tax-return preparation, be sure to provide him or her with all the necessary information.

If you are an owner and/or manager of a business and the CPA is required to work on company premises, be sure to demonstrate open support of the CPA, and encourage the cooperation of all company personnel. Be available to assist the CPA with any questions or problems that might arise, and assign someone to coordinate and produce any materials needed by the CPA, such as invoices, books of account, and other financial records.

Provide a suitable work environment for the professional staff of the CPA firm, such as a private office or a conference room. This is necessary because the professional staff may often handle confidential business records, such as payroll information and files on customer accounts. Also, a private work environment will enable the CPA to conduct interviews and meetings with company management and personnel free of distractions.

If the CPA's engagement entails an audit, review, or compilation of financial statements, try to schedule the engagement as close as possible to the year end, when financial data is more readily accessible and important accounting transactions are still fresh in people's minds.

Another way to work effectively with your CPA is to keep

organized records. There is no ideal way to maintain financial records, provided they make sense to you and the CPA who will need access to the information. Plain manila folders designated for specific items—sales invoices, payroll tax returns, travel expenses, medical expenses, and charitable contributions, for example—are useful in organizing records.

In most cases, canceled checks and bank-deposit slips constitute the bulk of financial records for businesses and individuals. These should be arranged in monthly order along with the related bank statements and an up-to-date checkbook or check register.

Working in close cooperation with your CPA should minimize some of the time needed to complete the task. The result should be a savings in the fee the CPA charges for services.

7

FEES FOR CPA SERVICES

The fees charged by CPAs generally follow a pattern similar to those for other types of professional services (legal, medical, etc.). A CPA's fees are seldom fixed; rather, they usually correspond with the prevailing economic climate. Fees for a CPA's services normally rise during an inflationary economy, and as the cost of living rises.

In the accounting profession, fees are not uniform. A large public accounting firm may have a higher billing rate than an individual practitioner because the larger firm has more overhead, such as the development of educational materials for clients and professional staff. As is true of most fees for professional services, fees charged by CPAs are often negotiable.

When CPAs structure their fees certain factors are considered, including any or all of the following:

- The time required to complete an engagement.
- The extent of the CPA's association with the engagement or the degree of responsibility assumed. For example, the CPA's responsibility with respect to audited financial statements is greater than his or her responsibility with respect to reviewed or compiled financial statements.
- The value of the CPA's expertise. For example, resolution of a complex estate-tax problem may require extensive research and result in a large fee.
- Availability of client company's personnel to provide assistance during the course of an engagement to gather financial records and prepare supporting financial statement schedules.
- Maintenance of office facilities (e.g., rent, office supplies, salaries of professional and clerical staff).
- Liability insurance required by the accounting firm.
- Continuing professional education taken by the professional staff.
- Competitive position with other accounting firms.

Cost of the service is the prime consideration when choosing an audit, review, or compilation. Because a CPA performs a limited number of procedures during a review or a compilation of financial statements as compared to an audit, less time is required to complete a review or a compilation. A review service generally requires 50 percent of the time required for an audit, while a compilation might require about 35 percent. For example, assume you are the executor of an estate and a set of personal financial statements is required in order to settle the estate. A CPA estimates that an audit will require 30 hours to complete. If the CPA charges you $85 per hour, the audit would cost $2,550. On the other hand, a review would cost approximately $1,275 (15 hours x $85), while a compilation would cost approximately $892.50 (10½ hours x $85).

Some factors are more important than others to certain public accounting firms. The time required to complete an engagement is probably the most important factor regardless of firm size. This is because billing rates are generally applied to the hours required to complete an engagement for a client. Those hours are referred to by CPAs as "chargeable hours."

Accounting firms have standard billing rates for each professional staff person. These rates take into account an individual's salary level, years of experience, and any specialized skill. Billing rates vary among professional levels within an accounting firm. Professional levels within most firms include staff accountants, seniors, managers, and partners or shareholders. As you might expect, the billing rates are pegged to the professional level of the person performing the service.

The range of fees of public accounting firms often varies with the prominence of the firm and the types of clients served. CPAs serving middle-income taxpayers and small businesses typically charge from $75 to $175 per hour. This fee range may vary depending upon the location of the CPA firm, where the cost of living may vary. For example, hourly rates for a CPA in New York City might be $150, as compared to $80 for a CPA in Atlanta, Georgia. It might cost you $300 to have an income-tax return prepared by a New York City CPA, while a comparable return might cost $180 when prepared by an Atlanta CPA.

A CPA firm operating from Long Island, New York, with a large taxation practice generally charges clients between $300 and $1,000 to prepare an income-tax return, which includes a $50 charge for expenses and hourly fees ranging from $80 to $100 per hour. If the firm takes five to eight hours to prepare an income-tax return, it might charge $800 to an individual earning close to $100,000 annually who also has dividend and interest income, some stock transactions, limited-partnership investments, and itemized deductions. On the other hand, a client with income only from wages and a small amount of investment income (e.g., less than $200 interest income) and some itemized deductions might pay the firm's minimum fee of $350. In general, the fee charged depends on the complexity of the tax return.

When discussing fees with CPAs, inquire as to the following:

- A description of the benefits to be received from the CPA's services,
- An estimate of the hours required to complete the engagement,
- The hourly or daily (per diem) rate to be charged,
- How the CPA arrives at the fee,
- Any out-of-pocket costs relating to the engagement (e.g., travel and lodging), and
- Billing procedures (e.g., monthly, quarterly).

8

SIZE AND LOCATION OF THE CPA FIRM

When choosing a certified public accountant, consideration should be given to the size of the accounting firm, and its location in relation to the home of an individual and/or the business facilities of a company. This Key provides some guidelines on these matters.

Size of Firm. A public accounting firm may be a sole practitioner, a partnership with firm members designated as partners, or a professional corporation with firm members as shareholders. Those forms of business may vary with respect to the number of professional staff who serve clients.

A small CPA firm includes a sole practitioner without any professional staff accountants or perhaps with one or two accountants working toward their CPA certificate. CPA firms with fewer than twenty professional staff accountants, which may include one to four partners or shareholders, are generally considered small.

Medium-sized firms are generally defined as having twenty to fifty professionals, and large firms ordinarily have over fifty professionals. Some medium-sized and large firms operate from more than one office, and may have several partners or shareholders depending on the nature and extent of the firm's practice.

Because of size, certain firms have distinct advantages. For example, small and medium-sized firms have the following advantages over large firms:

1. Provide more individual and personal attention to specific accounting, financial reporting, and taxation problems.
2. Concentrate on services relating to reviews, compilations, write-up and bookkeeping tasks, and tax-return preparation.

In general, small and medium-sized public accounting firms are close to their clients, often involving social and community relationships. Some people find this close business relationship desirable. A small or medium-sized public accounting firm is ideal for an individual, and for a business that has one base of operations, such as a retail store, restaurant, gas station, or a small manufacturing company. This also applies to companies with operations in a few locations, provided that the accounting firm has offices and staff near those locations.

A CPA firm with fewer than ten professionals should be capable of handling most individual needs, such as tax-return preparation, estate planning, and personal financial statements. In most cases, a firm of this size with appropriate experience and expertise can also handle accounting services for small businesses.

A highly specialized accounting firm is one that comprises at least four partners, each with responsibility over one of the following areas: accounting and auditing, taxation, management advisory services (MAS), and overall administration of the firm. A firm with these four departments is usually well-equipped to handle any specialized service needs of its clients, both individuals and small-business owners. The administrative partner is often the managing partner of the firm, while the other three partners concentrate on providing technical assistance to clients on accounting, auditing, taxation, and MAS matters.

Location of Firm. A major consideration in choosing a CPA is the location of the firm's offices. Proximity to company facilities has the advantage of minimizing the cost for a CPA's services. CPAs generally charge clients for out-of-pocket expenses, such as travel and lodging. If the CPA firm is located close to the company's base of operations, these out-of-pocket costs will be lower.

Businesses should determine whether or not the CPA can be readily available to visit the company location if necessary. If the company is decentralized, with operating facilities in various locations, the ideal is to engage a public accounting firm with offices close to company facilities. In this way, a representative of the CPA firm can be readily available at all locations and can foster a closer business relationship.

9
PRACTICE-MONITORING PROGRAM

If you require financial statements for your individual or business needs, one of the most objective criteria for evaluating the competence of a CPA firm's accounting and auditing practices is whether the firm is enrolled in a *practice-monitoring program* approved by the American Institute of Certified Public Accountants (AICPA). In order to retain membership in the AICPA, certified public accountants who practice in the United States or its territories are required to be proprietors, partners, shareholders, or employees of public accounting firms enrolled in an approved practice-monitoring program. To meet this requirement, CPA firms have two options:

1. The peer-review program of the AICPA Division for CPA Firms (membership is voluntary) or
2. The quality-review program.

Peer Review. Peer reviews are basically audits of accounting practitioners (i.e., CPAs) by other accounting practitioners (i.e., "peers"). A peer review focuses on the system of quality control for a public accounting firm, and is intended to determine whether that system is appropriately comprehensive and suitably designed relative to the firm's organizational structure, policies, and nature of accounting practice. Peer review concentrates on the following nine areas or elements of a quality control system:

- Implementation of a firm's independence requirements.
- Assignment of personnel to engagements.
- Consultation on technical problems.
- Supervision of field work on engagements.
- Hiring practices of the firm.
- Continuing professional development and education programs.

- Advancement of professional personnel.
- Client acceptance and continuance.
- Inspection of the firm's accounting and auditing work.

The results of a peer review are communicated by a written report issued by the peer reviewer. In most cases, the reviewer also issues a letter of comments that provides an explanation of deficient areas in the reviewed firm's quality-control system and recommendations for corrective actions. Where there is a need for remedial action, the CPA firm is expected to indicate in writing (i.e., a letter of response) its plans to correct the deficiencies. Peer-review documents are available from the public file of the AICPA Division for CPA Firms.

Quality Review. The second type of practice-monitoring program for CPA firms is quality review. All firms that are not members of the AICPA Division for CPA Firms are required to enroll in the quality-review program and submit to a review of their accounting and auditing practices every three years.

The objective of the quality review is similar to that of a peer review. However, there are some major differences between the programs. For example, the primary focus of a quality review is the quality of audit, review, and compilation engagements for small CPA firms—firms with fewer than ten professionals—while the peer review focuses on firms with eleven or more professionals.

Another major difference between the programs concerns the maintenance of reports. Peer-review reports and related documents are kept in a public file at the AICPA Division for CPA Firms. Reports on the results of quality reviews are evaluated by a Quality Review Committee of the CPA state society that administers the review, and strict confidentiality on the review results is observed. These reports can be obtained only from the reviewed firm.

Evaluating Review Results. The results of a peer review or a quality review should be an important factor in choosing a CPA firm. A firm that has been through either type of review, and has passed by receiving an unqualified report, very likely complies with the highest standards of the public accounting profession. Ask the firm you are considering whether it has participated in either practice-monitoring program and request a copy of the report on the review and any other related documents, such as a letter of comments and the firm's letter of response. Read the documents and ask the CPA to explain any matters that are unclear.

Although the practice-monitoring program is designed to ensure quality control over a public accounting firm's accounting and auditing practices, an effective system of quality control generally affects other CPA-related services, such as taxation. In other words, if a CPA firm improves quality over its accounting and auditing services, that quality should spill over into other services, especially where a CPA provides more than one type of service for a particular client.

Most CPA firms use the results of a peer or quality review as a selling point in soliciting business from a prospective client. Evaluate those results when choosing a CPA firm.

10

PROFESSIONAL IMAGE

The image that a public accounting firm projects to its clients and the general public is an indication of the quality of services one might expect from the firm. In order to obtain a clear perspective on a CPA firm's professional image, consider the following:

- Quality of personnel, which includes the levels of professional staff (e.g., partners, managers, seniors, junior staff) and the number of CPAs on the staff.
- Participation in continuing professional education.
- Legal suits against the firm.
- Practice development activities.
- Advertising.

Find out whether or not the majority of accountants associated with the firm are certified public accountants. Individuals who remain in public accounting for any length of time eventually become CPAs. If the majority of a public accounting firm's professional staff are CPAs they probably have been trained to render quality work for their clients.

Determine whether the public accounting firm undertakes continuing professional education (CPE) for its professional staff. CPA state licensing authorities have a mandatory CPE requirement, which is usually 120 hours of CPE over a three-year period. CPE requirements are usually fulfilled through training and educational programs conducted within or outside the firm, such as seminars sponsored by CPA state societies and the American Institute of CPAs. Continuing professional education enables CPAs to reinforce their technical knowledge and remain current on rules and standards relating to auditing, compilation and review, financial accounting and reporting, taxation, and management advisory services. A public accounting firm that encourages CPE for its staff helps to maintain standards for its clients.

Ask a prospective CPA if there are any pending legal suits against the accounting firm. Legal suits may arise from faulty or unethical practice, or related misunderstandings. Like doctors and lawyers, CPAs maintain insurance to protect themselves against malpractice suits. Determine whether or not the accounting firm has adequate malpractice insurance.

A public accounting firm communicates its philosophy through practice-development activities such as membership in the AICPA and CPA state societies, providing seminars on technical areas to clients, participating in technical committees of CPA state societies and the AICPA, and writing articles for professional publications. Ask about the firm's approach to practice development. In most cases, large firms are more active in practice development than smaller firms.

Larger public accounting firms are inclined to spend more on advertising their services as compared to smaller firms. Most advertising by CPA firms is communicated in good taste. However, be wary of any firm using an advertisement that knocks its competitors or claims to employ only experts on certain business matters within the community.

To obtain a good understanding of a public accounting firm's image, visit the firm's office; "audit" the facilities. Does the office appear to be a professional environment? Engage in conversations with the professional staff. Do they appear reasonably happy in their association with the firm? The environment in which professional accountants work is an indicator of professional image.

11

PROFESSIONAL ORGANIZATIONS AND CODE OF CONDUCT

There are professional organizations that coordinate and monitor the activities of CPAs and provide rules, regulations, and guidance in the carrying out of CPA-related services. These professional organizations, some of which were referred to in previous keys, include the American Institute of Certified Public Accountants (AICPA), various state societies of CPAs, and other CPA-related associations. Although these organizations are designed to serve their members directly, they also serve as a buffer between CPAs and their clients.

American Institute of CPAs. The American Institute of Certified Public Accountants is the national professional organization of CPAs. This group includes certified public accountants engaged in public accounting, industry, the government, and in the academic environment. The AICPA is structured to accomplish the following objectives:

1. Provide the public accounting profession with a broad range of programs designed to maintain and improve the quality of CPA services.
2. Promote and maintain standards of practice.
3. Enable the public accounting profession to contribute the business knowledge, experience, and skills of AICPA members who are CPAs along with other organizations that are active in accounting and related fields.

In general, the AICPA provides its membership with technical standards and guidelines and educational programs. The AICPA also keeps the public informed about the accounting profession, serves as spokesperson for accounting practitioners, and provides a forum for its membership to discuss issues affecting the practice of public accounting.

State Societies of CPAs. State societies of CPAs are designed to achieve objectives similar to those of the AICPA, except that membership is restricted to CPAs who practice within the state or territory of the society's jurisdiction. In general, state societies serve its members as follows:

1. Promote high ethical standards and technical competence.
2. Provide continuing professional education.
3. Address questions on technical matters relevant to accounting, ethics, liability, and other concerns.
4. Increase public awareness of the accounting profession.
5. Sponsor a comprehensive structure of technical committees.

Most state societies of CPAs are governed by a board of directors, and also conduct programs and operations through volunteer CPAs and a full-time and/or part-time staff.

CPA-Related Associations. There are also a number of professional associations made up of CPA firms rather than individual CPAs. These firms may be sole practitioners, partnerships, or incorporated firms. Like the AICPA and state societies, CPA-related associations provide educational and technical guidance for CPAs and serve as a forum for addressing technical issues faced by CPAs when servicing clients.

Code of Professional Conduct. The public accounting profession is governed by a Code of Professional Conduct, which provides ethical and performance standards for certified public accountants, and focuses on what CPAs should do to best service their clients. Devised and monitored by the American Institute of CPAs, the Code includes a number of rules and interpretations of those rules. Areas covered by the Code include independence, integrity and objectivity, general standards (e.g., professional competence and professional care in carrying out CPA-related services), compliance with professional standards, accounting principles, confidential client information, contingent fees, advertising, commissions, and form of practice.

For example, Rule 101, "Independence," requires CPAs to be independent in fact and in appearance. Independence in fact implies objectivity on the part of the CPA when performing accounting and auditing services, while independence in appearance implies freedom from any potential conflicts of interest that might lead someone to question the CPA's independence in fact. For example, if the CPA is involved in business transactions with a client company being audited, and is related through family bloodlines to an officer of that company, the CPA's objectivity may be compromised. In this case, independence in fact would be questioned.

Rules and related interpretations of the Code are not etched in stone. They are continually evaluated by jurisdictional groups in the American Institute of CPAs and in state societies of CPAs, and are subject to change.

The Code of Professional Conduct is also written to protect the public against any wrongdoing by a CPA. If you have a justifiable complaint against a CPA for any unethical business practice, a complaint may be registered with the Professional Ethics Division of the AICPA. The Ethics Division interprets and administers the Code of Professional Conduct. When a complaint is found to be justified, the Ethics Division can discipline members administratively, or summon them before a joint trial board, which has the authority to acquit, admonish, suspend, or expel a member from the AICPA. If warranted, the joint trial board can also seek the revocation of a CPA's license by appealing to the state licensing board of accountancy that granted the individual in question a CPA certificate.

12

ENGAGEMENT LETTER FOR CPA SERVICES

Since ambiguity often surrounds oral agreements, any contract involving the exchange of services for money should be in writing. If you engage a CPA to perform a service, obtain an engagement letter before the actual work begins. An engagement letter from a CPA is unnecessary when the service is only for the preparation of tax returns since the nature of that type of service is generally clear-cut.

Like other contracts, engagement letters are designed to protect the client and the CPA. An engagement letter provides the following advantages:

1. Establishes an understanding between the CPA and the client as to the nature and extent of CPA services to be rendered.
2. Indicates the fee for CPA services.
3. Reduces an oral agreement to writing.
4. Establishes a form of legal contract between the CPA and client as to their respective obligations.

An engagement letter also serves an individual or businessperson as a reference check for information that needs to be provided to the CPA before the actual work begins, such as the accumulation of any business records (e.g., bank reconciliations, paid checks, vouchers).

When accounting or other services are being provided for the first time, you should have the CPA orally explain the engagement letter. When you fully understand and agree with the precepts set forth in the engagement letter, sign it as an acknowledgment of the engagement and promptly return it to the CPA.

In most cases, one engagement letter covering services to be provided by a CPA for the year should be adequate—a letter covering compilations of quarterly interim financial statements and a review of the annual financial statements, for example. If these accounting services are to be repeated the following year, a new engagement letter should be requested for that year. Yearly engagement letters make allowances for any changes that might affect the business relationship, such as new or revised accounting pronouncements, revised tax laws and government regulations, and changes in business practices and management personnel.

A sample engagement letter follows:

Mr. and Mrs. Ralph Cramden
475 Norton Street
Trixieville, New York 10030

Dear Mr. and Mrs. Cramden:

This letter confirms our understanding of the terms and objectives of our engagement and the nature and limitations of the services we will provide.

We will perform the following services:

1. We will compile, from information you provide, the statement of financial condition of Ralph and Alice Cramden as of December 31, 19X2, and the related statement of changes in net worth for the year then ended, in accordance with standards established by the American Institute of Certified Public Accountants. We will not audit or review such financial statements. Our report on the financial statements is expected to read as follows:

> We have compiled the accompanying statement of financial condition of Ralph and Alice Cramden as of December 31, 19X2, and the related statement of changes in net worth for the year then ended, in accordance with standards established by the American Institute of Certified Public Accountants.
>
> A compilation is limited to presenting in the form of financial statements information that is the representation of the individuals whose financial statements are presented. We have not audited or reviewed the accompanying financial statements and, accordingly, do not express an opinion or any other form of assurance on them.

2. We will prepare the federal, state, and local tax returns for the period ending December 31, 19X2.

Our engagement is subject to the inherent risk that material errors, irregularities, or illegal acts, including fraud or defalcations, if they exist, will not be detected. However, we will inform you of any such matters that come to our attention. Our fees for these services will be $100 per hour, plus out-of-pocket expenses.

We shall be pleased to discuss this letter with you at any time. If these terms are acceptable to you and the services, as described, meet with your requirements, please sign this letter in the space provided and return it to us. A duplicate of the letter is enclosed for your records.

Sincerely yours,

_____

(Signature of CPA)

Acknowledged _____

Date

13

CHANGING YOUR CPA

Individuals and companies do not routinely change their public accountants. However, circumstances may dictate your having to decide whether the client-CPA relationship should continue.

As a matter of sound business policy, individuals and businesses should evaluate their CPA at least once a year in order to identify any factors or situations that might warrant a change to another firm. When deciding whether to continue to obtain the services of a CPA, consider certain matters, such as fees for services. For example, ask the following questions:

- Do the CPA's fees appear to be in line with the services that were provided?
- Are you notified in advance of fee increases, and are reasons for any increases thoroughly explained?
- Does the CPA provide some breakdown as to where time was spent on the engagement (e.g., procedures, report preparations, tax-return preparations) in conjunction with the submission of billings for services?

Another matter to consider when deciding whether to change your CPA is the timeliness of services performed. Ask the following questions:

- Does the CPA make early contact prior to the engagement?
- Does the CPA return telephone calls on a timely basis?
- If the CPA does not have an immediate answer to a particular question, is an answer provided within a reasonable period of time?
- Does the CPA provide periodic oral progress reports as to the status of the engagement?
- Has the CPA's work been completed on a timely basis (prompt preparation and delivery of tax returns, interim and year-end financial statements, etc.)?

A public accounting firm's "on-the-job" performance can

help you decide whether the firm should be retained for future engagements. Consider the following:

- Does the CPA attempt to educate the company on accounting and/or tax matters through conferences and/or discussions?
- Does the CPA appear to be interested in soliciting the views of responsible company personnel regarding strengths and weaknesses of the accounting system, and the short- and long-range goals of the business?
- During the course of an engagement, does the CPA indicate any of the following:
  1. Existence of deficiencies,
  2. The need for controls,
  3. Competence of the company's accounting staff?
- During the engagement, is the professional staff of the accounting firm courteous in dealing with company personnel and appear enthusiastic in their work?
- Does the professional staff appear to be properly supervised and work as a team?
- Does the CPA encourage joint meetings with company owners or management, and bankers?
- Does the CPA review the financial statements, accountants' reports, tax returns, and other related documents with you when those items are in draft form?

After completion of the engagement, two additional questions need to be addressed:

- Does the CPA continue to maintain contact after the engagement is completed (e.g., four-to-six-week intervals)?
- Does the CPA return financial records?

After the engagement is completed, a CPA should not retain your financial records for an undue period of time. In two separate instances in Pennsylvania, CPAs failed to return records to their clients.

In addition to losing the clients, both CPAs were found guilty of violating the Code of Professional Conduct of the Pennsylvania Institute (i.e., state society) of CPAs. As a result, they lost their membership in the state society and in the AICPA.

Depending on your circumstances, some of the questions raised in this key may warrant more attention than others. However, if there are negative answers to many of these questions, it may be time to seriously consider changing your CPA.

Another significant factor that warrants consideration for changing your CPA is whether or not the public accounting firm appears to be approaching insolvency. For example, during the past few years some public accounting firms have experienced lawsuits. As a result, some firms have gone out of business. A recent example is Laventhal & Horwath (L&H), a public accounting firm that filed for bankruptcy November 21, 1990. Business deals that went "sour" and corporate bankruptcies led many investors to bring legal action against CPA firms, such as L&H, in an attempt to recover investment losses that were precedented on investors' reliance on the audited financial statements of troubled companies.

Litigation against your CPA firm might be a clue that the firm is approaching insolvency. To determine if there is any pending legal action against your CPA, do the following:

- Read local newspapers for news items.
- Maintain contacts with business associates, bankers, insurance agents, and other professionals who network with law firms.
- Contact the CPA firm's state board of accountancy that granted the CPA firm's partners or shareholders a license or certificate to practice public accounting, and inquire as to any allegations against the firm.
- Contact the local state society of CPAs which often tracks any alleged misconduct of state society members.

If litigation leads your CPA firm into bankruptcy, like that of the L&H situation, you might be left with incomplete CPA services. Before you decide to sever a relationship with a CPA because of pending litigation against the firm, discuss the matter with your CPA. Since we live in a litigious environment, litigation also is sometimes based on unfounded allegations.

14

ASSESSING THE NEED FOR A FINANCIAL PLANNER

Whether or not you need the services of a financial planner depends on factors such as income level, the nature of financial goals, and time available to devise strategies for achieving financial goals. Regardless of age, if your yearly income-tax payments exceed 10 to 15 percent of your gross income, a consultation with a financial planner is warranted to consider tax-planning strategies.

A financial plan may cost from $250 for a simple computer-generated plan, to $2,500 or more for a comprehensive and more sophisticated plan. It is not cost-effective to use a planner if your savings are less than $20,000. With a little research, you can safely allocate those dollars to certificates of deposits, money-market funds, and/or mutual funds.

Individuals who have savings of more than $20,000 may benefit from the advice of a financial planner. The most important consideration when assessing the need for a financial planner is the nature of your financial goals, which may encompass any of the following:

- Providing for the education of children.
- Accumulating assets for retirement.
- Protection against personal risks through adequate insurance.
- Planning an estate for the family.
- Reducing the burden of taxes.
- Formulating an investment portfolio that generates adequate returns on investments.
- Planning for positive cash flow and maintaining an appropriate budget.
- Devising plans for starting and conducting a business.

Most of us do not have the expertise to accomplish these types of financial goals on our own. Career and family demands make it almost impossible to spend the necessary amount of time with important financial matters. If you aspire to one or more financial goals and lack the necessary expertise or the time to devote to financial planning, you might consider consulting a financial planner. For example, an architect from the Midwest had two children who were two years apart in age, both of whom wanted to go to college. The parent was faced with the prospect of paying from $15,000 to $25,000 each year for four to six years of college, depending upon the schools the two children selected. A financial planner helped the architect with the key objectives in the educational planning process: 1) determining the costs, 2) finding the money, and 3) devising a cash-flow strategy. In projecting the cost of education for both children, the financial planner took into account the inflationary increases that were bound to occur over that period of time.

If you own and operate a small business, a financial planner can provide assistance as a consultant. For example, a businesswoman in California consulted a financial planner when her retail store faced quarterly sales-tax bills. The planner recommended that she put cash in a money-market fund to be used whenever sales taxes are due for payment.

Assume that you want to protect yourself and your family from risk. A financial planner can help you find answers to the following questions:

- How much money would be needed in the event of a major loss such as death, disability, illness, or loss of property?
- What is the extent of financial loss that my family can endure, and for how long a period of time?
- How much cash flow can I spare to ensure against major losses?
- What is the extent of potential losses of my property?

Another financial objective might be planning for retirement. A competent financial planner can help you determine how much and when money will be needed, and how that need will be funded. A financial planner can do the following: make an evaluation of the available sources of retirement benefits currently available, devise assumptions as to possible rates of return, and determine the impact of inflation on any accumulated retirement earnings. An executive of a small insurance company engaged a financial planner to develop an individual preretirement plan. Satisfied with the overall plan and the strategy used to achieve the executive's retirement goals, he hired the planner to develop a preretirement program for his employees that evolved into a 401-k plan.

A financial planner should pursue three objectives for you:

1. Set realistic financial goals.
2. Devise strategies to achieve those goals.
3. Help in the implementation of these strategies.

All three objectives need to be focused within your available resources, some of which are wages, savings, and investments. Consideration should also be given to spending habits and patterns.

For example, a financial planner who is a vice-president in a major brokerage firm conducts seminars on financial planning. She disapproves of using income as a guide in determining the need for a financial planner, and poses the following questions to her seminar audiences:

- Do you have three to six months' take-home pay in a savings account or other form of liquid asset readily convertible to cash?
- Do you know how much and what kind of insurance you need, and have you purchased this coverage?
- Do you have a retirement plan and are you contributing to it on a regular basis?
- Do you know what percentage of your income you spend for necessary expenses, and do you earmark discretionary funds for various specific future financial goals?
- Are you saving for your children's education?
- Do you have a will?

These questions address matters that require some kind of financial planning. If you can answer "yes" to most of them, a financial planner may be unnecessary. On the other hand, if answers to most of the questions are "no," you should seriously consider consulting a financial planner.

By taking a complete inventory of your financial situation, a financial planner can provide a long-term diagnosis of your financial health. In this way, a financial plan will be developed that will enable you to live comfortably, within your means, and help you achieve your financial goals and security.

15

REFERRAL SOURCES FOR FINANCIAL PLANNERS

There are several referral sources to consider to find a financial planner that will help you achieve specific financial goals. The first source is referrals from friends and business associates whose judgment you trust. Query friends who have used a financial planner and find out whether they are satisfied with the services. Business associates, such as accountants, attorneys, bankers, and insurance agents are also an excellent source of referrals because these professionals often work closely with financial planners on financially related engagements. A referral from someone you trust is often the best method for finding a good financial planner.

Another source is your local telephone directory. Refer to listings under the following headings: financial adviser, financial consultant, financial planner, investment advisory services, and investment securities. Bear in mind that anyone can place an advertisement for rendering specific services. Whether or not they are qualified to provide those services is another matter.

If you cannot obtain recommendations from friends or business associates, your next step is to consult the various financial planning trade associations and the organizations that accredit financial planners. These professional groups are a good referral source because their goals are to establish and maintain professionalism in financial planning, promote continual education and advancement of knowledge in the field, and support programs designed to help financial planners better serve their clients.

By contacting the appropriate professional organizations or associations, you can find names, addresses, and telephone numbers of financial planners who conduct business close to you. Some of these organizations are the following:

- *International Association for Financial Planning (IAFP)*—Headquartered at Two Concourse Parkway, Atlanta, Georgia 30328, the IAFP is one of the oldest and largest associations whose members include financial advisers in all fifty states who, for compensation, provide advice to a client regarding strategies and actions to achieve financial goals based on an analysis of the client's capabilities, resources, and personal and financial condition. The IAFP provides its members with education, training, and ethical standards, and builds public and industry awareness of the need for professional advice. All members are required to subscribe to a Code of Professional Ethics, and may also participate in the Registry of Financial Planning Practitioners, an IAFP program encompassing certain education and experience requirements (see Key 18). The Registry provides the public with a consumer referral service of qualified financial planners.
- *The Institute of Certified Financial Planners*—Located at 7600 East Eastman Avenue, Denver, Colorado 80231-4397, the Institute represents over 7,000 financial planning professionals who have earned the designation certified financial planner (CFP) (see Key 18). Its objectives are similar to that of the IAFP, which also includes adherence by its members to a Code of Ethics. In order to assist consumers who wish to work with a certified financial planner, the Institute provides CFP referrals to the public.
- *The National Association of Personal Financial Advisers (NAPFA)*—Headquartered at 1130 Lake Cook Road, Buffalo Grove, Illinois 60089, NAPFA is the largest nationwide organization of fee-only financial planners. NAPFA's eligibility standards encourage its members to obtain the education, knowledge, and experience necessary to provide comprehensive financial planning to the public. Most NAPFA members have extensive experience in financial services, and possess professional designations such as: certified financial planner (CFP), certified public accountant (CPA), chartered financial analyst, juris doctorate, or master of laws. All NAPFA members are registered as investment advisers with the

Securities and Exchange Commission (SEC). Also, all NAPFA members must adhere to a Code of Ethics, bylaws, and other NAPFA rules and regulations. Most of the fifty states have NAPFA members, a list of which can be obtained from the Association.

- *American Institute of Certified Public Accountants (AICPA)*—Located at 1211 Avenue of the Americas, New York, New York 10036, the AICPA is the national professional organization of certified public accountants. (See Key 11.) The AICPA's Personal Financial Planning Division sponsors a program where a CPA can become an Accredited Personal Financial Specialist (APFS). (See Key 18.) Many AICPA member certified public accountants have attained the APFS designation and are qualified to provide financial planning services.

16

THE SELECTION PROCEDURE

In selecting a financial planner, choose three to five candidates for interviews. This will enable you to accomplish two objectives: 1) ascertain the background, experience, and competence of the individuals, and 2) learn what the planners can and cannot do for you. These objectives can be achieved with the help of the information covered in the remaining keys and the use of the interview questionnaire in Appendix B.

Remember that a financial planner cannot be an expert in all areas of financial planning. A planner often consults with other professionals, such as stockbrokers and/or insurance agents. Find out whether the planner follows an outside consultation approach when servicing clients.

The initial interview with each planner should be free of charge and might take approximately one hour. Try to schedule the meeting at the planner's office to get a feel for his or her professional surroundings and, more important, to make sure that the planner does not operate from a telephone and a post office box number.

If the interview takes place at the planner's office, ask to see a sample financial plan recently prepared for a client, preferably for a client whose goals are similar to yours. If the planner refuses because of the confidentiality of the client's name, ask if the client's name can be blocked out. If the planner continues to refuse, terminate the interview and move on to the next candidate.

To save time during the interview, the planner may want to review his or her files for an appropriate plan and forward it to your home, where you will have time to review the planner's work.

When you review the sample plan, do not be easily swayed

by cosmetic features, such as a leather-bound cover or fancy script-type print. If the plan contains technical jargon and terms, and does not appear to focus on the client's financial goals, return the plan with a polite thank-you note and consider another planner.

If the planner claims to be an investment adviser registered with the Securities and Exchange Commission (SEC), ask to see a *Form ADV*. As investment advisers, financial planners are required to file an ADV form, which discloses the following information about the adviser:

1. The nature of the adviser's business.
2. The background education and experience of key personnel in the adviser's firm.
3. Any disciplinary history.
4. The amount of assets under the adviser's management and the types of clients serviced.
5. The kinds of investment advisory services provided, and
6. The methods of securities analysis used by the adviser.

Another important matter that requires discussion at the initial interview is the planner's fee. The planner should give you some idea of the approximate cost of the services to be provided and any out-of-pocket expenses.

Ask the planner for references from clients with objectives similar to yours. The planner should also be willing to furnish you with references from other professionals he or she has worked with, such as bankers, insurance agents, lawyers, and stockbrokers.

At the completion of an interview, a planner may request that you fill out a questionnaire and return it to the firm even though a final commitment to do business has not been made. If the planner appears to be a likely candidate, the questionnaire should be completed. The information provided by a completed questionnaire will enable the planner to find out more about your income, net worth, and specific goals, and design a plan to suit your needs. A completed questionnaire also enables a planner to arrive at a precise cost for the service, which may hinge on the amount of your net worth.

17

CLUES TO COMPETENCE

In addition to professional credentials, a financial planner should have adequate work experience and possess knowledge in some specialized financial-related areas. Other considerations for choosing the right financial planner include the type of clientele serviced and the size and location of the planner's firm.

Experience. Consider a planner with no less than three to five years of financial planning experience. Anyone with less than three years of relevant experience might be considered a novice when it comes to handling the financial affairs of others. Another important factor is the planner's work experience before engaging in financial planning as a profession. Comprehensive personal financial planning encompasses investments, insurance, tax planning, and retirement planning. A financial planner should have five or more years of experience as an accountant, insurance agent, lawyer, or stockbroker. Experience in one or more of these professions equips an individual to handle a comprehensive range of financial planning services.

Specialization. Although most financial planners can help you meet a variety of goals, it is wise to choose one that specializes in the specific financial goal you are trying to achieve. For example, if you need advice on funding your child's college education, seek out a planner who is knowledgeable in all aspects of this type of financial aid. If your financial plan is geared toward retirement, select a planner who specializes in retirement planning and related tax-saving strategies.

Another rule of thumb is to consider a financial planner who has served others in your profession. Doctors, lawyers, and owners of small businesses often have specialized financial planning needs that can be fulfilled only by a planner who has worked for others with a similar professional background. A financial planner with experience and expertise in designing financial plans for people in specialized occupations is up-to-date on the latest developments in those professions. Based on their knowledge, these planners should be able to design a financial strategy to meet your professional and individual needs.

Size of Firm. There are certain advantages and disadvantages in working with an independent planner as opposed to a planner who is affiliated with a large firm. An independent planner with a small group of clients might be inclined to focus more attention on your account. Also, large firms have a tendency to devote more energy toward wealthy and corporate clients. On the other hand, a planner from a large firm generally has more resources at his or her disposal. If your financial plan calls for tax-saving strategies, a large firm can easily refer to its legal or tax department to check on the current status of changing tax laws. An independent planner, lacking those readily available resources, might have to do extensive tax-law research that could be time-consuming and costly to you if the planning fee is based on an hourly rate.

Most large firms also offer a wide variety of financial planning services, many of which an independent planner may be unable to provide because of a lack of expertise and research resources. On the other hand, a one-stop shopping approach for financial planning products may have surface appeal, but the financial plans of large firms often tend to favor certain products, such as investments in specific industries. Independent planners tend to provide a more personal approach to their service and are generally unbiased toward a specific product.

Location of Planner. You should consider a financial planner who has serviced clients in your community. References for a local planner can be easily checked. More important, the planner is likely to be familiar with the community's economic climate and the impact that the local economic situation might have on your particular financial plan.

18

PROFESSIONAL CREDENTIALS

A financial planner need not be an expert or specialist in all areas of financial planning. However, he or she should be knowledgeable in the following areas: debt management, estate planning, insurance, investments, retirement planning, and tax planning. Experience and knowledge in these fields are attained through a variety of educational processes, including college education, curriculum for a professional designation (e.g., CPF, ChFC), and/or continuing education.

By checking the professional credentials of a prospective financial planner, you will be on the right track for selecting a qualified professional. When choosing a physician, you generally look for the letters "M.D.," which signifies a board-certified doctor or physician. In like manner, look for designations that indicate whether a financial planner has passed rigorous tests and training that qualifies him or her as a financial planner. The remainder of this key discusses the various designations to look for. When you choose a prospective financial planner, he or she should possess at least one of these credentials. However, some planners have been in business for many years and are highly experienced, but have not obtained these credentials.

Certified Financial Planner (CFP). Most certified financial planners (CFPs) have earned a four-year college degree in an area such as accounting, economics, business administration, marketing, or finance. All such planners have completed the CFP educational program that is administered by the International Board of Standards and Practices for Certified Financial Planners (IBCFP). Headquartered in Denver, Colorado, the IBCFP is an independent, nonprofit organization that oversees the administration of the CFP comprehensive certification examination process and grants qualified individuals the CFP designation. In order to be licensed by the IBCFP as a certified financial planner, an individual must meet the following requirements:

- Successfully complete the IBCFP's comprehensive certification examination program, which tests knowledge on various key aspects of financial planning.
- Acquire one to five years of financial-services experience in a related field (such as banking or insurance), the experience needed depending on the level of college education the individual has reached.
- Adhere to the IBCFP's Code of Ethics, which covers objectivity, competence, fairness to clients, confidentiality, and professionalism.
- Obtain 30 hours of continuing education every two years in financial planning areas.

Financial planners prepare for the IBCFP examination by enrolling in the College for Financial Planning in Denver, Colorado, which provides a correspondence course that takes two to three years to complete. The course work encompasses the following subjects: fundamentals of financial planning, risk management and insurance, investment planning, income-tax planning, retirement planning and employee benefits, and estate planning.

Chartered Financial Consultant (ChFC). The ChFC title is conferred by the American College in Bryn Mawr, Pennsylvania. A ChFC candidate must successfully complete a comprehensive curriculum of college-level courses from the American College, which include fundamentals of financial planning, income taxation, individual life and health insurance, investments, estate planning, wealth-accumulation planning, financial planning applications, and retirement financial decision making. It takes four to five years to complete this program, which can be taken on campus or through a correspondence course of study. In addition to the course work, a candidate for the ChFC is required to have a minimum of three years' experience in the financial-services industry, adhere to the College's strict Code of Ethics, and enroll in the College's formal continuing education program, called Professional Achievement in Continuing Education (PACE). The PACE program requires a ChFC to take 60 credit hours every two years by attending programs that cover the following:

- Financial and retirement planning.
- Taxation and estate planning.
- Life, health, and disability insurance.
- Accounting and actuarial science.
- Pensions and employee benefits planning.

Chartered Life Underwriter (CLU). The American College also provides a correspondence or on-campus program for financial planners who may wish to specialize in either life insurance planning or personal insurance planning. To be designated a chartered life underwriter (CLU) by the College, a candidate must complete both the life and personal insurance curriculums, which entails:

1. Completion of insurance and financial planning courses.
2. Three years of business experience in the insurance industry.
3. Adherence to the College's Code of Ethics.
4. Enrollment in the PACE program.

The American College also sponsors the American Society of CLU & ChFC.

Accredited Personal Financial Specialist (APFS). The APFS designation is awarded by the American Institute of Certified Public Accountants (AICPA) to certified public accountants who provide personal financial planning services to clients. To obtain the APFS designation, a CPA must meet the following requirements:

- Hold a valid CPA certificate from a legally constituted state authority (i.e., a state board of accountancy).
- Be an AICPA member in good standing.
- Have at least 250 hours of experience per year in personal financial planning activities for the three years preceding application for the APFS designation.
- Provide a written statement of intent to comply with all the requirements for annual reaccreditation, which includes taking at least 48 hours of financial planning courses every two years.
- Pass a comprehensive six-hour examination that covers the following areas: professional responsibilities, the personal financial planning process, personal income-tax

planning, risk-management planning, investment planning, retirement planning, and estate planning.
- Submit six references to substantiate working experience in personal financial planning.

The Registry of Financial Planning Practitioners. The Registry of Financial Planning Practitioners is a program formed in 1983 by the International Association of Financial Planning (IAFP), a worldwide, nonprofit professional trade association. The Registry is designed to promote excellence in the field of financial planning by setting professional standards, such as a Code of Professional Ethics, so that its members maintain high standards of technical competence, morality, and integrity. There are no actual licensing requirements, and financial planners voluntarily apply for the program. Membership in the Registry of Financial Planning Practitioners is more akin to an honor society than an academic designation.

In order to be admitted to the Registry, financial planning practitioners must undergo a thorough evaluation procedure which includes:
- Preparation of a comprehensive written application.
- Registration as an investment adviser with the SEC.
- Submission of an actual financial plan.
- Submission of references from five clients who have worked with the practitioner for two or more years—and who have received comprehensive financial planning.

A Registry member must have attained one or more of the following:
1. A designation, such as CFP, ChFC, and/or CPA.
2. A degree of juris doctorate or master of law.
3. A bachelor or a graduate degree in financial planning or in a related business area from an accredited institution.
4. Completion of a financial planning curriculum accredited by the Registry.

Members of the Registry must have practiced as a financial planner for at least three years and pursue financial planning as their primary vocation.

A member must also use the Registry's comprehensive financial planning process in order to develop a financial plan. Members of the Registry are required to pass a Practice

Knowledge Examination, which evaluates their understanding of the financial planning process and other general financial planning concepts. In order to maintain their status in the Registry, members must also complete 60 hours of continuing professional education credits every two years and provide the Registry with documentation on CPE completion.

If you engage a financial planner who possesses one or more of the credentials covered in this key, you can be reasonably assured that the services provided are based on ethical standards of practice. Adherence to such standards is incumbent upon financial planners who carry these professional credentials. As stated earlier in this key, there are some highly experienced financial planners who have been in business several years but who may not carry titles such as CFP, ChFC, CLU, etc., which have evolved over the past two decades. If a financial planner has been in business for over twenty years, before the various professional credentials became fashionable, you can usually be reasonably assured that he or she provides financial planning services with professionalism and integrity.

19

FEES FOR FINANCIAL PLANNING SERVICES

Financial planners charge for their services based on an hourly fee, commission, or a combination of the two. A financial plan may cost anywhere from $250 for a simple plan for an individual, to $2,500 or more for an intricate plan for corporate executives and small business people. It is imperative to discuss fee structure with financial planners.

Fee Only. "Fee-only" financial planners charge for services in any one of the following ways:

- An hourly fee ranging from about $50 to $300 per hour, based on the number of hours the planner works.
- A flat fee, which may range anywhere from $250 to $5,000, which is a designated amount for a specific service.
- A percentage fee, such as one to four percent of annual income or net worth.

In general, charges for a financial plan vary among fee-only planners. For example, a fee-only planner in Florida stated that she typically charges a flat fee of $250 to $1,000 for a financial plan. Another fee planner in Florida indicated that she may charge up to $4,000 for a financial plan, depending on its complexity.

The *fee-only* financial planner limits services to giving advice, and does not receive any compensation based on the implementation of recommendations to clients, such as sales commissions, referral fees, and reimbursed costs. The planner avoids potential conflict of interest in promoting investment products, and does not receive any personal gain from the implementation of investment recommendations.

Since a fee-only financial planner does not accept compensation other than fees, he or she can be expected to remain unbiased and work toward the best interests of a client. A fee-only planner tries to find the most appropriate investments for clients. For example, a middle-aged couple in Texas consulted a fee-only planner in Illinois who carefully weighed and recommended no-load mutual funds that resulted in lower costs and higher returns to the couple.

Another advantage of using fee-only planners is their approach to the financial planning process. In most cases, fee-only planners focus their attention on all areas of a client's financial situation, which may include investments, insurance, retirement, funding for education, and/or estate planning. A drawback to using a fee-only planner is the cost for the service, which can be substantial if the financial planner is used for future consultation and monitoring the strategy of the financial plan. If the fee is charged hourly, total cost for services may be especially high.

Commission. Some financial planners charge a commission on the investment products they sell, such as eight percent on a mutual-fund investment or four percent on a tax-shelter investment. In some instances, commission-only planners are affiliated with brokerage houses or specialty firms that deal almost exclusively in financial planning. These planners usually prepare a computer-generated plan at little or no cost to clients. The compensation for these planners is based on the investments they sell when the recommendations in the plan are followed by the client.

"Commission-only" financial planners are useful if your financial goal involves investments, because they afford the convenience of "one-stop shopping" for investment products. However, since these planners depend on selling specific investment products, they may not be as objective as fee-only financial planners.

Fee/Commission. Some financial planners charge a fee for a financial plan and a commission for the sale of products. The majority of financial planners fall into this category. In most cases, their fees are lower than those charged by fee-only planners. The fee/commission financial planner is similar to the fee-only planner with respect to objectivity. If your financial goals include investments as well as other areas, consideration should be given to using a fee/commission financial planner. Some financial planners accommodate clients by offering an option between a fee-only and a fee/commission payment structure. For example, a financial planning firm in San Francisco recently shifted from a commission-and-fee structure to one that allows its customers to choose fee-only or fee/commission arrangements.

Points to Ponder. When evaluating the fee structure of a financial planner, make certain that you will not be charged for any hidden or ambiguous costs. Find out, for example, whether a full hour will be charged for a five- or ten-minute telephone call by the planner. Also, if the fee depends on the amount of your net worth, make sure that the financial planner explains how net worth is defined. Net worth is generally what you own (e.g., cash, securities, retirement funds, cash value of ownership in a business, and the cash value of personal properties) less what you owe (e.g., mortgage debt, personal loans, credit card bills outstanding, and taxes due).

Finally, if the financial planner charges a commission for investments purchased, find out whether the commission schedule of the planner's firm is competitive with other firms that sell investment packages. In general, be certain that you know what you are paying for.

20

THE FINANCIAL PLANNING PROCESS

Although financial objectives differ from person to person, the process employed by most financial planners in developing a long-term strategy for your financial future is generally the same. After an initial meeting, where the financial planner explains the nature of services offered and you decide to engage those services, the financial planning process continues as follows:

1. The planner explains the financial planning process, compensation for his or her services, and the documents and data required for developing a financial plan.

2. The planner provides you with a checklist of required forms and documents needed for developing an appropriate plan. You compile the documents and complete the forms as accurately as possible.

3. The planner reviews and analyzes your financial position, which entails identifying financial goals and objectives. In this way, the planner helps you to clarify financial and personal values and attitudes, which may include providing for a child's education, supporting elderly parents, and providing for retirement.

4. The planner identifies any financial problems that might impede your financial goals and objectives, such as inadequate or excess life insurance coverage, inadequate cash flow to meet expenses, or an investment portfolio unsuited to your financial needs. The planner assesses a profile for you that should encompass both rewards and risks that might result from following a certain course of action.

5. The planner develops a profile that might include ideas from other advisers (e.g., an insurance agent or a lawyer). The profile encompasses a review of alterna-

tives, strategies, and investment or financial options to consider. Recommendations to achieve your objectives are formulated. The planner meets with you to discuss the results of the plan. You can provide feedback to help in fine-tuning the final plan.

6. The planner prepares a written financial plan designed to meet your financial goals. If you approve the plan and any further modifications, you may decide to also use the planner's services to implement the plan.

If so, then the following occurs:

7. The planner assists you in implementing the plan, which includes coordinating with other professionals such as insurance agents, stockbrokers, and lawyers.

8. The planner monitors the progress of the plan and, based on his or her review and evaluation, advises you of any factors that might affect that progress, such as changed economic conditions. At this point, the planner also notifies you of any needed changes to the financial plan.

This process encompasses the basic service that should be provided by your financial planner in return for the fee. Depending upon the complexity of your financial goals, certain steps in the process may require more concentration than others.

A financial planner in South Carolina generally holds four conferences with clients, which may take from one to three hours each, before completing a comprehensive financial plan that costs $3,500 to $5,000. In addition, there may be other conferences with the client's accountant and attorney.

21

ENGAGEMENT LETTERS

To ensure that your financial goals and expectations coincide with the financial plan designed by the planner of your choice, the planner can prepare an engagement letter. In this way, misunderstandings and/or uncertainties between you and your planner may be avoided. An engagement letter guides the planner in focusing attention on your financial goals.

The engagement letter should cover the following points:

- The services to be provided.
- Your role in the process (e.g., compiling information for the financial plan).
- The financial objectives of the plan.
- A description of any limitations concerning the financial advice, such as guarantes of results from investments.
- The amount or basis upon which the planner's fees will be charged.

The planner's services should be described in detail. This is important, because a general description of services might be misinterpreted by you to include services that were not contemplated by the planner.

In some cases, a financial planner may list services in the engagement letter that will never be performed, in order to impress you about the nature and extent of his or her expertise.

Carefully scrutinize the services listed in the engagement letter to make sure that your needs are properly addressed, and be certain that the planner has not indicated the performance of certain services you do not need.

An example of an engagement letter follows:

Mr. and Mrs. Hugh R. Rich
711 Dollarwise Avenue
Greenbucks, N.C. 10062

Dear Mr. and Mrs. Rich:

This letter sets forth our understanding of the terms and objectives of our engagement to provide comprehensive personal financial planning services to you. The scope and nature of the services to be provided are as follows:

Review and Evaluation

We will review and analyze financial information furnished to us relating to your current financial circumstances which will include: current investments, retirement planning, income-tax planning, insurance coverage, and estate planning.

Written Plan

Based on our review, we will prepare a written analysis of your current financial situation. We will also prepare, in writing, specific preliminary recommendations that will seek to address your financial goals. Where appropriate, we will include financial illustrations and projections for greater understanding of the potential outcomes of financial alternatives.

We will meet with you to discuss our analysis and will provide you with a preliminary draft copy. You will be given an opportunity to concur with the preliminary recommendations or suggest modifications. Following agreement on your personal financial goals and the strategies to be used to achieve them, we will provide you with a final version of the plan.

Implementation

We will assist you in implementing the agreed-upon strategies. Accordingly, we will be available on an ongoing basis, by telephone or in person, to answer questions, to assist you or your other advisers to take necessary actions, and to make recommendations regarding financial matters.

Monitoring and Periodic Review

We will maintain records of your investment assets to monitor the progress toward achieving your financial goals. As economic and market conditions change, we will initiate suggestions for changes in your portfolio. From time to time, we may bring to your attention actual or anticipated changes in tax law that we believe may affect your situation.

At your request, we will review your potential investments, based on the offering materials and financial projections provided, and discuss with you whether they appear to be appropriate for achieving your objectives. Our analysis will include consideration of the potential impact of existing or anticipated tax law on anticipated results.

As needed, we will prepare income-tax projections for the current tax year and suggest tax-planning strategies geared to your individual needs and circumstances.

Limitation on Scope of Services

These services are not designed, and should not be relied upon, as a substitute for a client's own business judgment, nor are they meant to mitigate the necessity of a client's personal review and analysis of a particular investment. These services are designed to supplement the individual's own planning and analysis and aid the individual in fulfilling his or her financial objectives.

In addition, these services are not designed to discover fraud, irregularities, or misrepresentations made in materials provided to us concerning existing or potential investments. These services do not include other services which may also be provided upon request by us or other professionals, including but not limited to any one or more of the following: (1) tax-compliance services, including tax-return preparation, (2) legal documents such as pension plans, wills, trusts, or other agreements and contracts, (3) review and analysis of the offering materials of potential tax-shelter investments provided to us by you, and (4) any other service not specifically addressed in this letter.

Client Responsibility

It is not possible to provide comprehensive personal financial planning services without necessary information made available to us on a timely basis. By indicating your acceptance of this engagement, you agree to provide us with requested information and documents, such as financial statements, tax returns, summaries of investment accounts, wills, trust documents, insurance policies, information concerning employment and retirement benefits, etc. You also agree to advise us with duplicate copies of your monthly statements of activity and portfolio holdings.

Fees for Services

Our fee for these services will be based on our standard hourly rates and the number of hours required. Your fee for the first year will be a minimum of $_____ and will not exceed $_____. We will bill you in four quarterly installments, with the first installment due upon acceptance of this engagement. The fourth payment will be adjusted to reflect actual time expended, not to exceed the maximum total amount quoted for the year.

Term of Services

The initial engagement for comprehensive personal financial planning services outlined in this letter covers the one-year period beginning _____ and ending _____. This engagement may be terminated by you at any time by written notice to us. Upon receipt of such notice, we will prepare and forward to you a bill for our time expended to date.

If this letter correctly sets forth your understanding of the terms and objectives of the engagement, please indicate your concurrence by signing in the space provided below.

Sincerely yours,

_____
(Signature of Financial Planner)

The above letter sets forth my understanding of the terms and objectives of the engagement to provide comprehensive personal financial planning services.

_____ _____
Date   Signature of Client

22

COMPILING ESSENTIAL INFORMATION

Compiling all of the relevant information is important. The essence of financial planning is to know what data is important and how that data should be utilized. As a client, it is your responsibility to provide the necessary information to the planner. Failure to provide complete and thorough data prevents the planner from performing the engagement satisfactorily. If the data is incomplete, there is a danger that the planner may offer inappropriate advice with regard to the financial plan.

Most financial planners provide their clients with a questionnaire or checklist designed to elicit certain information they will need to devise a plan. As mentioned in Key 16, this is usually done at the initial meeting. In the meantime, you might gather some essential information so that it is accessible.

Set up a record-retention procedure, which might include desk drawers, file cabinets, file folders, or whatever works best for you. Whatever device is used, maintain copies of the following:

- Federal and state income-tax returns for the past several years (i.e., at least five years).
- Federal gift-tax returns filed over the past few years.
- Any data or documentation on businesses owned, such as partnership agreements or articles of incorporation.
- Financial statements on individual family members and on businesses owned.
- Agreements related to testamentary disposition such as wills, trusts, divorce, stock redemption, etc.
- Real estate data (e.g., location, date purchased, cost basis, fair market value, etc.)

- Breakdown of income from all sources (e.g., wages, interest, dividends, etc.)
- List of all assets owned, including purchase dates, mortgages, etc.
- Contracts and/or plan descriptions for employee benefits, such as pension plans, profit-sharing plans, deferred compensation plans, and group insurance.
- Insurance policies relating to life, disability income, car, home ownership, etc.

All of this information may not be necessary, depending upon the nature and objective of the financial plan. However, such information should be made available if the financial planner needs it.

23

THE FORMAL
FINANCIAL PLAN

The financial planner's recommendations will be presented in a *written* format or plan to eliminate any uncertainty about his or her advice resulting from the engagement. A written financial plan ensures that the planner's advice has been thoroughly considered with respect to risks and rewards associated with the financial objectives.

Depending upon the complexity of the plan, a written financial plan takes from one to three months to prepare. The plan includes a profile of your current net worth (i.e., assets, or what you own, minus your liabilities, or what you owe), an analysis projecting future income and expense, as well as the planner's recommendations.

The number of pages in a financial plan can vary. A comprehensive plan covering strategies relating to an estate or retirement plan might range from 20 to 80 pages. However, a plan should not be judged based on its volume. The important factors are that the plan is tailor-made to meet your financial goals and needs, and that it is clear and concise.

The most important aspect of any financial plan is that goals and objectives are *clearly spelled out* and are not too general. For example, a doctor practicing in Kentucky spent $1,000 for what he thought would be an in-depth financial plan. The plan he received was an eight-page report on computer printout that addressed only the most general of recommendations.

Carefully review the financial plan, and do not hesitate to ask the planner questions about ambiguous or unclear items. Make sure that the document thoroughly covers the subject matter. For example, a financial plan on estate planning should identify the assets included in your estate, and an analysis of the control, disposition, and taxation of those assets. This should include: 1) estimates of estate value, and

2) estimates of federal estate tax with calculations that indicate the total amount passed on to your heirs after your death and the death of your spouse.

This type of plan should also cover an elementary understanding of estate planning techniques and *specific* recommendations for shifting assets so that you and your spouse can take advantage of estate-tax credits. There should also be some reference within the plan to your will.

Bear in mind that a good financial planner may not necessarily be an expert on estate planning, insurance, or stocks. The financial plan will be a *basic outline* for estate planning, insurance needs, investment options, etc. The financial planner is responsible for coordinating with other professionals and documenting that coordination. For example, if the plan relates to insurance needs and the planner is not an insurance agent, an agent should be consulted about automobile, disability, health, homeowner's, and life insurance. The financial plan should include the recommendations of that insurance agent.

Financial planners who are members of the *Registry of Financial Planning Practitioners* (the Registry) are required to adhere to certain standards. One of those standards is that a comprehensive financial plan contain certain elements. Although the order and style of presentation may vary, the Registry requires that a financial plan contain the following:

- **Personal Data**—Relevant personal and family data for those covered under the plan.
- **Client's Goals and Objectives**—A statement as to the client's financial objectives, including priorities and any time frames for achieving those objectives.
- **Identification of Issues and Problems**—All relevant issues and problems identified by the client, planner, and/or other advisers, which may include educational costs, taxes, major illnesses of family members affected by the plan, and other factors.
- **Assumptions**—Material assumptions used in the preparation of the plan such as inflation, investment growth, and mortality.
- **Balance Sheet/Net Worth**—A presentation and analysis including, but not necessarily limited to, a schedule of

assets and liabilities, along with a schedule of net worth and itemized schedules of assets and liabilities, where appropriate.

- **Cash-Flow Management**—Statements and analysis including, but not necessarily limited to, a statement of the client's sources and uses of funds for all relevant years, indicating net cash flow and an income statement.
- **Income Tax**—An income-tax statement and analysis that shows projected income taxes for all years covered by the plan.
- **Risk Management/Insurance**—This should include an analysis of a client's financial exposure relative to mortality, liability, and property, including business; and a listing and analysis of current policies and problems including, but not limited to, life, disability, medical, business, property/casualty, and liability.
- **Investments**—A listing of the client's current investment portfolio, and analysis of the liquidity, diversification, and investment risk exposure of the portfolio.
- **Financial Independence, Retirement Planning, Education, and Other Special Needs**—An analysis of the capital that will be needed at some future time in order to provide for financial independence, retirement, children's education, or other special needs, and a projection of resources expected to be available to meet those needs.
- **Estate Planning**—An identification of assets that are included in the client's estate and an analysis of the control, disposition, and taxation of those assets.
- **Recommendations**—The written recommendations of the plan should specifically address the client's goals and objectives. All issues and problems identified in the plan should describe actions that are necessary to compensate for any shortfalls in achieving goals.
- **Implementation Schedule**—A list of actions required to implement the recommendations, which should indicate priority actions, responsible parties, and timing of actions.

The plan recommended by the Registry covers many areas of financial planning. You may want to use the Registry's recommended thirteen-step format.

24

IMPLEMENTING AND REVIEWING THE PLAN

A well-designed financial plan is ineffective unless it is properly implemented. It is important to make sure that implementation occurs shortly after the plan is completed.

Since most financial planners are not necessarily specialists in all areas, they may not be able to implement all parts of the plan. As already mentioned, implementation may require other professional services, such as attorneys, CPAs, insurance agents, and stockbrokers.

The financial planner acts as a liaison between you and other professionals and supervises the implementation of the plan. Only a competent attorney should draft wills and trust agreements as part of an estate plan and only an insurance agent should provide advice on the right type and amount of insurance. The services of other professionals should be decided on at the outset of the engagement and should be addressed in the engagement letter and, of course, in the financial plan itself.

To monitor the degree of success achieved from the plan in meeting your objectives, the plan should be reviewed on a regular basis with the planner. This should be done at least annually, and preferably twice a year. At that time, the following questions should be addressed:

- Were plan expectations met?
- Are there areas where improvement is needed or certain areas that were not beneficial?
- Are there areas you are highly interested in or that were most helpful in achieving your financial goals?
- Are there additional concerns that should be met by the financial plan?

- Was the financial planning process worthwhile?

Depending on the answers to these questions, you may consider updating the original financial plan.

Throughout the implementation and review phases of the financial planning process, continue to work with the planner and other professionals of the financial planning team to accomplish your goals. Consult with the planner when necessary. Advise the planner of any changes that might affect your financial status, such as employment, residence, marital status, and health. A good financial planner will have your best interests at heart and will *enhance* or *maintain* your present financial situation. For example, a financial planner in Nashville, Tennessee, endeavors to develop a close working relationship with her clients so that they call her whenever they have extra income to invest, or whenever a family problem presents a financial obstacle, such as custodial responsibilities for an aging parent.

25

REGULATION OF FINANCIAL PLANNERS

Financial planners are not subject to government regulation. However, the Investment Advisers Act of 1940 requires that anyone who provides investment advice for compensation is required to be registered as an investment adviser with the Securities and Exchange Commission (SEC). According to the SEC, there is a significant overlap between *financial planning* and *investment advisory* activities. Most financial planners are registered as investment advisers under the Investment Advisers Act. There are some exceptions to the federal rule for registering with the SEC. For example, the registration requirement does not apply to the following:

- Financial planners or firms with fewer than 15 clients.
- Brokerage-firm salesmen who give financial advice on a commission-only basis.
- Certified public accountants who provide investment advice as an activity incidental to their regular services without receiving a fee for that advice, and who do not promote themselves as investment advisers or financial planners.

Registration with the Securities and Exchange Commission (SEC) does not imply that the SEC endorses that person as an investment adviser. When someone registers as an investment adviser, the SEC performs a background check on the individual to determine whether there are any records of criminal-fraud or securities-law offenses.

As a registered investment adviser, the individual is answerable to the SEC if he or she fails to perform investment advisory services in a responsible manner.

SEC endorsement is not a guarantee of the honesty and integrity of the planner. For example, in June 1991, the General Accounting Office (GAO) issued a report,

"Investment Advisers: Current Level of Oversight," which described a woman who lost her $60,000 life savings in a fraudulent investment scam perpetrated by a "financial planner" who was registered with the SEC as an investment adviser.

Approximately 37 states also require that anyone who provides investment advice for a fee be registered as an investment adviser. State procedures are generally similar to those of the SEC.

Federal regulation of the activities of financial planners is under consideration by Congress. It would require all financial planners to register with the SEC and disclose information about their qualifications and sources of income. Also, legislation would enable consumers to sue financial planners for damages under certain circumstances. However, individual state legislatures might adopt regulatory rules for financial planners before the federal government does.

There are approximately 60,000 "financial planners" in the United States. The number of "investment advisers" registered with the SEC has increased from 4,800 in 1980 to 16,200 in 1989, which includes individuals as well as firms that have thousands of employees.[1] Until these professionals are regulated by federal or state governments, *you* are the best protection against incompetent financial planning. Self-regulation can be accomplished by careful scrutiny of credentials, education, experience, and other clues to a financial planner's competence.

---

[1] Morgan, Jerry, "Your Adviser Is Registered? Well Big Deal, So Is Your Dog," *Newsday*, October 14, 1990 (Mineola, New York).

26

CHANGING YOUR FINANCIAL PLANNER

Every year more and more individuals put out a shingle that says, "financial planner." Although only a handful of them are con artists, each year this small group is responsible for defrauding millions of dollars from investors. A study done in 1988 by the North American Securities Administrators Association revealed that, over a two-year period, 22,000 investors lost $400 million to con artists posing as financial planners. Every day, newspapers and magazines have horror stories about scams in which unfortunate people have been victimized by financial planners who have minimal skill and training, lose money through negligence and bad advice, sell bogus securities to generate income for themselves, and steal money outright. "Self-dealing" is pushing an investment product or service to benefit one's own self-interest rather than the client's.

For example, in Palm Beach, Florida, "financial planners" met with a number of people, most of whom were elderly, at a church-sponsored seminar. The planners convinced 21 seminar participants to invest $400,000 in promissory notes, and afterward diverted the money for their own use. In Texas, a "financial planner" defrauded hundreds of investors of more than $8 million through a complex loan scheme. One of the victims was a 70-year-old woman who lost her life savings of $185,000 and was forced to go back to work to support herself.

To prevent yourself from becoming a victim of the con artist who poses as a financial planner, watch for "red flags" that indicate the integrity of the planner and/or the service being sold is suspect. Avoid financial planners who do any of the following:

- Guarantee unusually high returns on specific investment products.

- Suggest that you withdraw your money from IRAs, 401-k plans, pension plans, and other tax-advantaged retirement accounts, and place those funds in investments chosen by the planner.
- Urge you to place all your money into a single investment that is "insured," "guaranteed," and/or generates "tax-free income."
- Suggests coming to your home, or meeting you at the bank to receive the money for an investment in a "rare opportunity."
- Tries to interest you in gems, rare coins, or art investments that are often difficult to appraise and monitor.
- Avoids discussing how he or she gets paid for services rendered.
- Offers few or no alternatives to an investment plan.
- Claims to be an "expert" in all areas of financial planning.
- Touts a canned computer-software product that produces an inexpensive financial plan.
- Provides a form of printout that makes specific projections for more than two or three years as to what your net worth might be if you follow the recommended financial plan.
- Encourages you to give him or her power of attorney and/or discretion over your bank account so that you will not have to be "bothered" whenever an investment opportunity arises.
- Quotes you a fee before becoming familiar with your personal situation and financial goals and needs.
- Sells financial planning products generated by only one company.

Also, beware of financial planners without a staff, especially those whose "office staff" is a telephone-answering service. Be wary of financial planners whose addresses are post office box numbers and who avoid giving you a street address. This type of planner moves rapidly from one post office box number to another and leaves behind a trail of bad advice and fraudulent investments.

Keep in mind that all of these "red flags" should be warning signs for staying away from other financial specialists as well—whether they are CPAs, stockbrokers, money managers, or financial planners.

If you suspect that you have been victimized by a "self-dealing" financial planner, register your complaint with the SEC if the planner is an SEC-registered investment adviser. Or find out if the planner belongs to any one of the professional associations described in Key 15. If your planner is a certified financial planner (CFP), contact the International Board of Standards and Practices for Certified Financial Planners (IBCFP), which oversees the certification of CFPs. (See Key 18.)

The SEC, professional associations of financial planners, and the IBCFP will impose disciplinary action on financial planners who demonstrate that they are unable to competently fulfill responsibilities owed to clients. For example, when grounds for discipline have been established, the IBCFP may impose any of the following on a certified financial planner (CFP):

- A letter of admonition to the CFP.
- A suspension of the individual's right to use the CFP designation for a period of time, but no more than three years. Publication in a press release or some other form of publicity about the suspension.
- Permanent revocation of an individual's right to use the CFP designation, the nature of which would be accordingly published.

27

MONEY MANAGERS AS COMPARED TO OTHER FINANCIAL SPECIALISTS

Like financial planners and stockbrokers, money managers are investment advisers, and many have a background in financial planning and brokering stocks. However, money managers differ from financial planners and stockbrokers in several respects.

For example, the range of services differ. Financial planners offer a wide variety of advisory services in areas relating to insurance, retirement planning, children's education, and estate planning. Stockbrokers buy and sell securities, as well as all other investment-related products at the client's approval. As an investment adviser, the money manager's job is restricted to *portfolio management*—overseeing portfolios of stocks and bonds as well as other assets. Financial planners and stockbrokers generally consult with the clients and receive approval before engaging in any investment transactions. However, accounts with money managers are *discretionary*—that is, the money manager buys and sells securities *without* the client's approval.

Financial planners and stockbrokers will handle accounts for both individuals and small-business owners with a few thousand dollars to invest. Money managers set minimum account size levels of $100,000 to $1 million per account, primarily servicing wealthy individuals and families. In most cases, the client's net worth is three to four times the amount of the account. Money managers also serve corporate clients, and many manage company pension funds and profit-sharing plans.

Financial planners may work independently or for firms such as insurance companies. Stockbrokers are usually employed by brokerage firms. Most money managers are employed by investment counseling firms or banks. They also may be affiliated with a brokerage firm as a separate subsidiary.

Financial planners and stockholders are paid primarily by commission; money managers are paid a *fee*. Most money management fees are calculated as a percentage of the total assets of a client's account.

Another major difference among the three types of professionals concerns regulation. Financial planners are usually certified by one or two national financial planning associations. Stockbrokers are governed by the various stock exchanges and the NASD. There are no associations that certify money managers.

The Securities and Exchange Commission has some regulatory authority over money managers. As investment advisers, money managers are registered with the SEC and file an *ADV form* in accordance with the Investment Advisers Act of 1940.

Another major difference concerns insurance. Under the Securities Investor Protection Corporation (SIPC), accounts with stock brokerage firms are insured up to $100,000. But neither SIPC nor any other organization covers accounts with money management firms.

Of course, because of the nature of discretionary accounts, consultation regarding trades differs between money managers and stockbrokers. Money managers spend less time on the telephone with clients because they do not *sell* anything and need not *explain* their trades to clients. The money manager's fee is based on the amount of assets under management and increases in line with growth in a client's net worth. A money manager does not make commissions, as a stockbroker does when stocks are traded. Unless money managers execute their own trades, they escape notice by the stock exchanges and the NASD. Most money managers use stockbrokers to execute their trades.

28

WHEN IS A MONEY MANAGER NEEDED?

You should consider a money manager if you have $100,000 or more to invest, lack sufficient time to make your own investment decisions, and are willing to wait (e.g., at least five years) to reap the rewards (or losses) of the money manager's investment strategy. The most fundamental benefit a money manager can provide is peace of mind in knowing that your money is being invested according to a consistent pattern of guidelines.

A money manager also performs certain administrative duties for a client, such as keeping track of dividend and interest checks, conferring with the client's accountant and attorney on matters such as the timing of tax losses, and liquidating a portion of holdings if the client needs to draw cash from the portfolio. A money manager should *not* act as a custodian of your account. This should be the responsibility of the brokerage firm or the bank that employs the money manager. In this way, the money manager does not have ready access to your funds, but only directs those funds by selecting the appropriate securities for your portfolio.

A money manager tailors your portfolio to suit your tolerance for risk, while trying to achieve certain investment goals. It is important that you not balk at the first downturn of the stock market during the period of time you engage a money manager. Continue to ride the stock market's waves in bull and bear markets. As a result, you will improve your chances of receiving the long-term returns that the stock market is known to confer upon the patient investor.

If you are a doctor or other professional running your own practice, a money manager can serve both you and your business. For example, a surgeon practicing in South Carolina hired an investment counseling firm to manage a $100,000 profit-sharing plan for himself and his staff. The surgeon and the money manager assigned to his account had compatible investment philosophies—to protect the principal sum invested and search for stocks in undervalued industries. Under the money manager's direction, the profit-sharing fund nearly doubled after five years. The performance of the profit-sharing fund prompted the surgeon and his wife to engage the money manager in investing $60,000 of personal assets that were formerly kept in a low-yield money-market fund. Eventually, the personal account earned a gain of 32 percent, which at the time compared to a 16 percent increase in the S&P 500 index. By engaging a money manager, the surgeon was able to focus on his medical practice and use the extra time to enjoy his family and hobbies.

If you are an entrepreneur operating a business, a money manager can also serve your business and personal financial goals. For example, a president of an advertising agency in Jackson, Mississippi, was dissatisfied with his agency's profit-sharing plan. The plan was being managed by a local bank that placed most of the funds into bonds used to finance new church buildings. Although it appeared to be a safe investment, the interest income generated by the bonds was not competitive with other bond and equity investments. After engaging a money management firm to control the profit-sharing plan, the plan's assets began to grow within a year. As a result of this experience, the president of the ad agency engaged the firm to manage both his and his parents' personal assets. He was able to concentrate on his business instead of the time-consuming task of managing two personal portfolios.

In another instance, a Los Angeles couple, after receiving $100,000 from the sale of a condominium, hired a money manager to invest the proceeds from the sale since they knew nothing about investing. This arrangement allowed the couple to concentrate on the husband's commercial-photography business while the money manager focused on enhancing the couple's investment portfolio. Within a few years, the couple's portfolio account earned an average of 20 percent a year.

29

THE FORMAL INVESTMENT POLICY

If you decide to use the services of a money manager, an *investment policy statement* should be prepared that will enable you to accomplish the following:

1. Assess your financial and personal characteristics and investment objectives.
2. Enhance your ability to evaluate the money manager's performance.
3. Coordinate communications between you and the money manager.

In general, an investment policy statement documents the goals of your investment portfolio and the guidelines to be followed by the money manager to achieve those goals. The statement should be long-term in nature, and should be responsive to the needs for which it is intended—for example, to accumulate funds in order to retire with a comfortable income at a certain age.

It should *not* dictate the management structure of the investments in the portfolio because that is the job of the money manager. The investment policy is used as a *guide* by the money manager to shape the investment portfolio that will fulfill your specific long-term needs.

A well-constructed investment policy statement addresses the following:

- A clarification of your financial position, which summarizes your balance sheet (i.e., assets and liabilities) and income prospects, including any potential volatility of your personal circumstances or business. This might include vulnerability of your business to foreign competition or the potential effect of inflation on your income.
- A clarification of your investment attitude or tolerance for risk. For example, if you have a maximum tolerance for

any percentage declines within a given period of time, it should be stated in the investment policy. You might consider a statement such as: "A loss of 10 to 20 percent of value in any two-month period exceeds my loss threshold." In this way you caution your money manager to retain a substantial amount of cash in your portfolio that is not subject to cyclical conditions of the stock market. The most important consideration is that your risk tolerance is not inconsistent with your investment objectives or with the practicalities of investing over the long term.

- Any limitations on the *quality* of your investment portfolio that might limit the actions of your money manager. You may wish, for example, to exclude investments that relate to any one or more of the following: small growth-oriented companies, holdings of unlisted stocks, certain industry groups, foreign securities, private placements, initial public offerings (IPOs), and options. In any event, limitations on your portfolio should be considered with care so as not to unduly restrict your money manager's discretion.
- A description of any maximum-size holdings by security, such as ownership of any particular stock at cost and a certain percent at market. For example, if you have a low tolerance for risk, you may want to limit 20% of the stock in your portfolio to companies in new or growth industries.
- The amount of discretion to be allowed the money manager, such as responsibility for only a portion of personal assets.
- The extent of communications between yourself and the money manager (e.g., frequency of phone calls and meetings).

An investment policy statement does not have to be etched in stone. In other words, you can draft a preliminary statement before selecting a money manager, and review the document with the manager of your choice. With this approach, the money manager will have a road map for directing your investment objectives.

30

FINDING THE RIGHT MONEY MANAGER

The most common way to find a money manager is through referrals from friends, business associates, accountants, financial planners, insurance agents, and stockbrokers. Money managers can also be found at most national and regional stockbrokerages and in the trust departments of banks. You can also check your local telephone directory under "Investment Advisory Services." Another way to find a money manager is through the services of investment management consultants, "talent scouts" who track and recommend money managers for a fee.

Investment management consultants track the investment or performance records of money managers, matching investors with the top performers. They select money managers in the same way money managers select high-performance stocks. Most consultants look for average annual returns of about 20 percent from the money managers they recommend. For example, a consultant from Springfield, Massachusetts, searches for money managers with a track record ranging from 17 to 22 percent over a 7-to-10-year period. Another consultant affiliated with a firm in Birmingham, Alabama, recommends money managers who have earned 16 to 27 percent for their clients over a ten-year period. Some consultants are affiliated with brokerage firms, while others are independent.

In general, a consultant can assist you by:
- Establishing an investment policy statement as well as an asset-allocation plan that follows the policy.
- Deciding on the money management styles suitable to your needs.
- Evaluating and selecting the right money manager for you.
- Monitoring the performance of your money manager and the account being managed.

In exchange for matching a client with a money manager, a consultant may charge a trading commission. Most consultants charge a flat fee for selecting a money manager and an additional fee for monitoring the money manager's performance.

Based on this monitoring, the consultant advises a client whether to continue engaging the money manager's services. For example, a well-known consultant in San Diego, California, charges a flat fee of $1,500 to select a money manager, and $500 a year thereafter to monitor the manager's performance and recommend whether the manager should be retained or dismissed.

As the consultant monitors the performance of the money manager, the client receives a quarterly performance report. Throughout the monitoring process, the consultant looks for investment consistency and checks up on personnel changes at the money management firm to ensure that responsibility for managing the portfolio hasn't been shifted to a less experienced manager.

Referrals for independent consultants can be obtained by writing to the Institute for Investment Consultants, P.O. Box 6123, Scottsdale, Arizona 85261. Members of the Institute must have 25 accounts totaling at least $15 million. They are also required to employ a specific and detailed procedure to assist a client in selecting a money manager.

Although the fees for an independent management consultant are high (at least $1,500), it is worthwhile to consider one if you have a substantial amount of money to be managed. Many of these consultants also work as financial planners. If you decide to use an investment management consultant, choose one who has at least five years' experience in selecting and monitoring the performance of money managers and derives at least 50 percent of his or her income from providing this service.

31

MONEY MANAGEMENT FEES

A money manager who has an impressive succession of high-performance years can often command higher fees from old as well as new clients. Money management fees are also a function of the *size* of an account. Larger accounts generally command lower money management fees. In this way, a commitment to buy money management services is similar to borrowing money. The more money you have available for managing by a money manager, the less it costs for the managerial service.

Fee schedules of money managers often average from one to 10 percent of assets annually. They may be based on a sliding scale or on a flat fee. The sliding-scale fees *descend* as the account size increases. In other words, in the first year a money manager might charge you two percent of total assets. If the account grows within a certain period of time (e.g., five years) as a result of the manager's investment strategy, the fee may slide down to one percent of total assets.

A money manager who charges a flat fee may accept any account size, but will usually set a minimum fee (e.g., $5,000). On a $1-million-dollar account, a minimum fee of $5,000 would be only one-half of one percent of the account. But on a $100,000 account, the minimum fee of $5,000 represents five percent of the account.

The larger your account becomes, the more the money manager earns on that account. For example, if your total investment portfolio grows from $1 million to $3 million in five years, the fee slides down from two percent the first year to one percent the fifth year as a result of asset growth. But the money manager's fee increases from $20,000 in year one to $30,000 in year five. Therefore, your money manager works to make your account grow in a timely manner, both to ensure a better return on your assets and to obtain a larger fee for managing your portfolio. Regardless of the size of your account, you are also required to pay the brokerage commissions on the securities the manager buys and sells for you.

When comparing fees among money managers, do not be enticed by lowball fees, which may reveal something about the firm's organization and investing style. For example, a firm with low fees may have to service more accounts than a firm that charges higher fees and may be unable to give your account the required attention. If a firm assesses low fees but has too many clients, the end result may be mediocre performance.

Another question to consider is whether a firm charging low fees has the money to spend on sophisticated research and computer capabilities, which are often essential to generating high investment performance. On the other hand, money management firms that charge high fees (i.e., over one percent of total assets) have "high expectations," in terms of increased rates of return on the portfolio, that may prove to be unrealistic. This could result in high turnover of accounts, and excessive time devoted to marketing money management services rather than to portfolio management.

Money management services are similar to anything else you buy. In other words, you get what you pay for. If the fee is high, the money management firm should demonstrate superiority in attaining performance results. Although fees are important, they should not be the sole consideration in selecting a money manager. The major concern should be the probability of strong performance in the growth of your portfolio.

If you are using an investment management consultant in obtaining a money manager, you might be offered a *wrap-fee* arrangement, which entails a variety of investment-related services, such as:

- Services provided by the consultant in selecting and monitoring a money manager.
- Overseeing your portfolio by the money manager.
- Transaction and custodial costs relating to your portfolio.

Wrap-fee arrangements are generally provided by consultants who work for brokerage firms. Instead of the traditional fee structure, in which payment is made for each service provided by the consultant, money manager, and stockbroker, you pay one fee for all services. Wrap fees, which can pose an annual cost of one-and-a-half to three percent of total managed assets, are more common for individual accounts than company or institutional accounts.

A wrap-fee arrangement is beneficial if you expect your money manager to heavily trade your portfolio. In this way, you save on brokerage commissions that may add up as a result of heavy trading. On the other hand, if you expect less-than-heavy trades by your money manager, brokerage commissions and the money manager's fee will probably amount to less than a wrap fee.

32

PROFESSIONAL ASSOCIATIONS

Money managers registered as investment advisers with the SEC may also work as financial planners and be members of one or more financial planning associations (see Key 18). At least two associations cater exclusively to money managers and investment counseling firms:

- The Association for Investment Management and Research (AIMR) and,
- The Investment Council Association of America (ICAA).

Your money manager or investment counseling firm may be a member of one or both of these associations.

Association for Investment Management and Research (AIMR). The AIMR is a nonprofit organization located in Charlottesville, Virginia, that is designed to promote standards of competence and professionalism in the practice of investment management and research. The group provides certain services to portfolio managers, securities analysts, consultants, and other investment specialists. AIMR members have bachelor's degrees from an accredited academic institution or equivalent education, or work experience in an investment-related field such as investment counseling, banking, brokerage, or insurance.

The association provides its members with a number of programs and services relating to the following:

- *Code of Ethics*—Members are required to adhere to the AIMR's Standards of Professional Conduct and annually file a Professional Conduct Questionnaire with the Association, disclosing any complaints made against them concerning professional conduct. Any violations of the Standards may result in sanctions against members ranging from a private reprimand to a revocation of AIMR membership.

- *Continuing Education*—AIMR provides a continuing-education program for its members that includes seminars, workshops, and publications on investment topics.
- *Certification*—AIMR coordinates a program that awards the Chartered Financial Analyst (CFA) designation to investment professionals who demonstrate their competence by passing three, six-hour examinations that cover the following areas: financial accounting, quantitative analysis, economics, fixed-income securities, equity securities analysis, and portfolio management. CFA candidates must also have a minimum of three years' experience in the investment industry.
- *Guidelines for Professional Practice*—AIMR representatives meet on a regular basis with representatives from regulatory groups, such as the Securities and Exchange Commission, the Financial Accounting Standards Board, and other national and state regulatory and legislative bodies to establish performance standards that will serve as a model for the investment industry.

Investment Council Association of America (ICAA). The Investment Council Association of America (ICAA) is a professional association of investment counseling firms ranging from small firms to large organizations with several hundred employees. ICAA's objective is to establish and encourage professional and ethical standards among its members. To qualify for membership, an investment counseling firm must be in business for at least a year and have a requisite number of clients, requisite being at least 10 clients who are unrelated to the firm by bloodline.

ICAA members are kept up-to-date through periodic distribution of educational and guidance materials on subjects relating to fidelity bonding, recordkeeping, and legal and regulatory matters. The Association, located in New York City, also interfaces with regulatory groups, such as the SEC, to enhance performance standards in the field. ICAA also sponsors special conferences for its members on timely topics relevant to investment counseling, such as performance measurement, administrative procedures, and data processing for investment-counseling firms.

To foster professionalism, ICAA formulated and adopted "The Standards of Measurement and Use for Investment Performance." This document provides guidelines and background information for many managers to use in compiling and using portfolio performance data.

Members of the Association must adhere to certain principles of conduct in the practice of investment counseling. These principles are codified in the "Standards of Practice for Member Firms." Some of these principles have been used by Congress and the SEC as the basis for legislation and regulations governing the conduct of investment advisers, and by the Supreme Court in defining the standards of fiduciary conduct for all investment advisers. Those standards cover the following:

- Professional responsibility.
- Professional qualifications.
- Financial responsibility.
- Compensation for services.
- Investment-counsel agreements.
- Promotional activities.
- Confidential relationship with clients.

33

REVIEWING EXPERIENCE AND PERFORMANCE

If you decide to find a money manager on your own, interview at least three candidates or investment counseling firms. Before checking further, find out their experience and performance, and what their minimum account size requirements will be. A money manager with an impressive track record might have a minimum account size of $1 million or more. If your account is substantially smaller than that, of course, you'll need to consider other candidates.

You should know something about the background and qualifications of the portfolio managers at each firm. This should include prior business experience, and personal and academic backgrounds of the manager or account executive who will handle your money.

One source of information is the manager's ADV form. As mentioned earlier, money managers are required to be registered with the Securities and Exchange Commission (SEC) as investment advisers and must provide certain information on the ADV, such as management fees, a description of the manager's investment strategy, educational background, and work experience. Ask the money manager for copies of parts one and two of the ADV. This document reveals whether a money manager has been the subject of an SEC lawsuit or any other problems. If the money manager has been in business for less than five years, check the ADV form to determine where he or she had prior experience with investments. Follow this with a query to the former employer as to whether the manager was responsible for making investment decisions.

Ask to see a written history that substantiates any claims to a solid past performance in managing client portfolios.

Examine the manager's performance record over at least the past five years, preferably on a quarterly basis, and compare it with benchmark indices such as the Standard & Poor's 500 stock index, the Dow Jones Industrial Average, or bond indices. These indices are available in back issues of *The Wall Street Journal*, the business section of major newspapers or at your local library. By reviewing performance numbers over a period of at least five years in comparison to an index, you should see performance for one full market cycle. Be sure to obtain performance figures on client portfolios that resemble the size and investment philosophy the money manager will oversee for you.

As a rule, a skilled money manager should at the least have beaten the S&P by one to three percentage points during bear markets such as 1971, when the S&P fell by seven percent, and 1981, when the S&P fell by five percent. As indicated in Key 30, investment management consultants generally recommend money managers who have attained a 20 percent annual rate of return. However, that rate should only be considered a rule of thumb, and might not apply to money managers who were able to guide client portfolios through bear markets such as 1973–74.

The performance figures provided by money managers should be audited and should include *all* accounts under management, not just an exemplary "paper portfolio." Performance figures should be *net results* after payment of management fees and trading costs, and comparable to an appropriate index such as the S&P 500.

Find out about the money manager's or investment counseling firm's investment philosophy and style to see if it is compatible with your investment goals and risk for tolerance. Some managers forecast market trends, then key specific industries, selecting certain companies in that field. Other managers ignore market trends and focus on specific companies at the outset, while others focus attention on broad subjects such as growth and then invest in companies they expect will show above-average earnings gains and high returns on equity.

For example, a money manager, who is the president and founder of his Boston-based investment counseling firm, favors investing in high-growth stocks such as high-tech companies. A chairman of a Los Angeles-based investment counseling firm, meanwhile, focuses on stable stocks and well-established companies. A New York firm utilizes a three-fold approach to portfolio management:

- Lose no more than 10 percent of a client's portfolio value in any one year.
- Beat the Standard & Poor's 500 stock index by two to four percentage points.
- Outpace inflation by at least six percentage points.

Performance information should include a list of securities purchased for clients in recent years. Find out whether the individuals who achieved the performance results are still with the firm. This is an important test in determining performance capability. The loss of key personnel could signal the end of a firm's success in obtaining good results.

As a general rule, avoid firms that manage over $500 million in assets. These large firms usually are not owned by individual money managers and usually cannot nimbly maneuver in and out of the market as well as a smaller sized manager. As a result, investment performance may at times be ineffective.

A money manager who handles a small portfolio can quickly sell most, if not all, of a portfolio's stocks when it is deemed inappropriate to remain in the market. For example, it is generally prudent to sell stock in a particular company when earnings for a 12-month period go below the earnings of the previous year, or when the stock's price falls by more than 10 percent.

If these situations occur, a manager with a small portfolio should be able to execute sales transactions with less market impact than an investment counseling firm that manages large portfolios for many clients.

You should also obtain the names and telephone numbers of a few clients serviced by the money manager. You can ask clients about their satisfaction with the money manager's performance, how often the manager reviews account performance, and the extent of the manager's responsiveness to questions raised by clients pertaining to accounts. Before engaging a money manager to oversee her portfolio, a retired dental assistant from Nebraska asked the money manager for six client references. Make sure that the money manager provides you with a few current clients—that is, clients who have been engaged by the manager within the past five years. More than likely, you will be provided with some of the money manager's best and most long-term clients. A review of current and long-term clients should give you a good feel for the manager's performance.

Prior to interviews, obtain the following information from the money management or investment counseling firm:

- Background and history of the firm.
- Minimum and maximum account sizes accepted.
- Total assets and number of clients being managed.
- Extent of staff's experience in portfolio management.
- Number of accounts per manager.
- Investment philosophy and style.
- Structure of the firm's decision-making process.
- Source of research.
- Schedule of fees.
- Compensation structure for personnel assigned to a portfolio.

With this type of information, and the use of the questionnaire in Appendix C, you should be in a good position to choose the right money manager to suit your temperament and time frame for achieving your investment goals.

34

MANAGING YOUR
MONEY MANAGER

After hiring a money manager or investment counseling firm, continuously monitor their performance. Carefully review all documentation you receive relating to the account. This should include:

1. Confirmations on all trades.
2. A quarterly statement listing the securities in the account, their market value, all purchases and sales for the period, and the market value of the account for the beginning and end of the quarter.
3. An annual detailed statement summing up the account.

Compare the return on the account with the S&P 500 or some other index. Give a money manager at least a year to prove his or her worth. If the manager's performance lags behind the S&P 500 index by five percentage points or more over one year, consider finding a new money manager.

Also, if the value of your portfolio holdings drops 20 percent from the high of the previous quarter and the money manager does not move your holdings into cash or decide on other remedial action, change money managers.

For example, an investment consultant in California was monitoring the performance of a money manager who performed well by buying stocks in small growth companies and then selling those stocks when they dropped 10 percent from their high. Eventually, the manager began to hold on to the stock of some companies that did not meet the 10 percent yardstick. This was a signal for the consultant to recommend that the client terminate the relationship with the money manager.

In another instance, a commercial photographer in Los Angeles makes it a practice to call his money manager whenever he gets a statement noting the purchase of a new stock for the portfolio. He then proceeds to question why the stock was bought and get some idea as to the money manager's expectations for the particular stock.

Meet with your money manager at least once or twice a year to review how your account is being handled. In general, accounts are reviewed by portfolio managers on an "as needed" basis. For example, an account may be reviewed daily, or at least weekly. It all depends on the circumstances of the market and the composition of your account.

When the market is active, accounts will be reviewed daily in order to determine what stocks should be bought or sold. If an account comprises mostly equity holdings, it will be reviewed more often than will a balanced portfolio of stocks and bonds that is less volatile to market swings.

When arranging meetings with a money manager, request an agenda of items to be covered, as well as recent performance statistics on your account. Meetings should cover the following areas:

- A review of your portfolio as compared to stated objectives.
- Reiteration of management style and philosophy.
- Discussion of any organizational changes within the firm, such as new account activity, minimum and maximum size of assets under management, and employee turnover.
- Changes in portfolio structure.
- Review of quality of earnings, average maturities, and marketability of securities based on the firm's research.

According to the Investment Advisers Act of 1940, an investment adviser registered with the SEC is required to furnish each advisory client with an annual written disclosure statement, which may be a copy of part two of its ADV form or a written document containing the information required by part two of the form.

Be sure to remind your money manager of this if he or she overlooks providing you the information. Review this information and compare it to information disclosed in the prior year's ADV form for any major changes, such as current problems or lawsuits with the SEC.

While monitoring your money manager's performance by reviewing relevant documentation and having periodic meetings, be alert to warning signs that indicate a troublesome firm. These signs or clues include the following:

- Another manager is assigned to manage your portfolio.
- Key employees leave the firm.
- Major clients terminate their relationship with the firm.
- Performance is below the major indexes, such as the S&P 500 or The Lehman Brothers Corporate Bond Index.
- Ownership of the firm changes hands.
- Telephone calls are not returned promptly, or the level of personal attention to your account appears to be lacking.

If you spot any of these situations, or hear about them through friends, business associates, and the media, discuss them with someone at the firm and find out why they occurred before deciding to terminate the money manager. A superior money manager will make a commitment to maintain the agreed-upon investment approach so that it coincides with the parameters of your investment objectives.

In light of market downturns, any one money manager cannot be on target all the time. Do not place too much emphasis on the performances of specific investments. For example, you might be disappointed with a 16 percent portfolio gain for your *diversified portfolio* compared to a 20 percent return on an equity index. In this type of situation, a valid comparison cannot be made. As a client, make sure that your money manager is adhering to the agreed-upon strategy, then assess the performance results with the appropriate index. In general, some money managers perform better in bear markets and others perform well in bull markets.

35

SETTING INVESTMENT GOALS WITH A STOCKBROKER

Before you begin searching for the right brokerage firm and stockbroker, make a decision as to what you want your investments to accomplish. This will help a stockbroker intelligently plan your investment program and help you achieve your investment goals.

As an investor, you may decide your major emphasis will be on potential growth, income, safety, or a combination of these. Some investment objectives are the following:

- *Long-term capital growth*—This goal is suitable for investors who want capital appreciation over a period of time in order to provide adequate funds at some future date for reasons such as children's education, purchase of a home, or a retirement fund.
- *Income*—This goal is for investors who desire some measure of safety when it comes to principal and liquidity in the event funds are required for an emergency or immediate need.
- *Short-term profits*—This goal is for investors who are willing to speculate and take risks considered to be above average in order to obtain a high return within a short period of time.
- *Tax savings*—This goal is for investors who seek tax-free income as a means of easing their current tax burden, and also shelter a portion of their income.

Your personal and/or business financial situation is the best guide to setting an investment goal. For example, if you have an adequate income that covers all living expenses with some dollars left over, and are also relatively young, you are in a position to take some risks for investment gains in the future.

In such cases, long-term capital growth might be an investment goal that is right for you. This goal would also apply if you are a successful businessperson with an investment program and additional funds to invest. You might consider speculative stocks or bond issues. The rationale for this investment goal is that you would not necessarily miss losing the invested dollars if these investments did not develop as intended. But if the investments did well, your reward would be significant capital appreciation.

On the other hand, if you are retired and live on a fixed income, your investment goals might be income and/or tax savings to obtain income from dividends and interest, at the same time protecting your principal. For example, an elderly widow who depends primarily on Social Security and the returns on her investments should focus her interest on stable income and preservation of principal. She would need "income securities," such as bonds, preferred stocks, and some high-quality "blue-chip" common stocks that return high dividends. She should not be concerned with long-term growth possibilities and would probably avoid speculative stocks.

A stockbroker can sell you various "investment packages" other than stocks and bonds. Most brokerage firms operate a retail type of service that includes investment packages such as limited partnerships, index options and futures, life insurance and annuities, mortgage-backed securities, mutual funds, and unit investment trusts. In general, the larger the firm, the more investment products it has to offer. For instance, Merrill Lynch, one of the largest national brokerage firms, has over a hundred investment products.

Whatever your investment goals, remember that there is risk involved with all investments. As a general rule, the greater the anticipated rate of return, the riskier the investment.

At the same time, many factors affect the prices of stocks and bonds, such as the U.S. economy, international economics, money and inflation rates, as well as conditions in a particular industry. Regardless of whom you choose as your stockbroker, that person does not have control over the factors that cause stock and bond prices to rise and fall.

Be sure that you can afford to lose the money. Also, have adequate life insurance and sufficient cash reserves.

36

INVESTOR PROTECTION OF ASSETS

Most people feel comfortable keeping their money in a bank with the knowledge that savings accounts are insured by the Federal Deposit Insurance Corporation (FDIC) up to $100,000 per account. If the bank fails, the FDIC provides some protection. But what if a brokerage firm fails? Is there recourse for investors who are clients of brokerage firms to recoup the money invested in stocks, bonds, and mutual funds?

Like the FDIC, which provides protection to bank depositors, the *Securities Investor Protection Corporation* (SIPC) provides a form of insurance for investors who are brokerage-firm clients. SIPC (pronounced "si-pick") is a nonprofit, membership corporation located in Washington, D.C., created by Congress to protect brokerage-firm clients. SIPC covers customer accounts when firms fail and are forced into bankruptcy. The limits of protection are $500,000 per customer. Claims for cash are limited to $100,000 per customer.

As a nonprofit corporation, SIPC is funded by its member broker-dealers. It also has a $1 billion line of credit from the United States Treasury. SIPC is composed of seven directors, five of whom are appointed by the President subject to confirmation by the Senate. The other two directors are selected by the Federal Reserve Board and the Treasury.

Members of SIPC are registered as brokers or dealers under Section 15(b) of the Securities Exchange Act of 1934, and are members of a national securities exchange, such as the New York Stock Exchange (NYSE), the American Stock Exchange (AMEX), or the National Association of Securities Dealers (NASD). Broker-dealers registered with the Securities and Exchange Commission (SEC), other than banks registered as municipal securities dealers, are automatically members of SIPC.

If the brokerage firm handling your investments fails, SIPC freezes your account and asks a federal court to appoint a trustee to liquidate the firm's assets. SIPC may protect the customers directly in cases where the brokerage firm is small. A notice of insolvency along with a claim form is sent out to customers which must be filled out and returned to the trustee. Both the trustee and SIPC may arrange to have some or all customer accounts transferred to another SIPC-member broker-dealer firm. If this is the case, customers are notified promptly and are allowed to deal with the new firm or transfer their accounts to another firm of their choice.

In situations where account transfers to another broker-dealer are not possible, SIPC will make sure that you receive all the securities registered in your name, or cash in an amount equal to the market value of those securities. An inability to transfer an account to another broker-dealer might occur when the records of the failed firm are inaccurate. If necessary, the trustee may buy new securities to replace those that were lost by the failed broker-dealer. After transfers are made, any remaining claims for damages or loss are subject to the $500,000 limit.

Of course, it goes without saying that SIPC does not insure the *outcome* of any investment. SIPC's sole function is to protect or safeguard investments from being jeopardized by financial difficulties encountered by member brokers and dealers. SIPC cannot and will not protect you from losses resulting from bad investment advice.

To determine whether a stockbrokerage is a member of SIPC, write to the Securities Investor Protection Corporation, 805 Fifteenth Street, N.W., Washington, D.C. 20005-2207.

37

FULL-SERVICE AND DISCOUNT BROKERS

A stockbroker acts as an *agent* on your behalf by executing buy and sell orders for stocks and bonds. Stockbrokers are generally categorized as "full-service" or "discount" brokers. Both types of brokers are similar in that they buy and sell securities for your account. However, the basic difference in service provided by each relates to information. A full-service broker provides investment ideas and gives professional guidance in buy and sell decisions. A full-service broker advises you about investments most suitable to your needs. A discount broker simply executes a client's buy and sell orders.

Generally, full-service brokers spend large amounts of money on research departments and analysts that do research on companies whose shares trade on stock exchanges. If you want information on a particular company, such as a prospectus or research report, a full-service broker usually accommodates your request. In return for extensive research and attention and service provided by a full-service broker, you pay a higher fee, usually up to double the price charged by a discount broker.

However, fees vary among full-service brokers and discount brokers themselves. Full-service brokers earn their fees from commissions. An average trade may have a charge that is 2 to 3 percent higher than the value of the transaction. The full-service broker then keeps 30 to 40 percent of that amount. If you are a small investor who trades infrequently, those trades may not generate much in commission dollars. Be aware that as a result the broker may not pay much attention to your account.

The prices charged by discount brokers vary according to the type of trading you engage in, the size of your order, and other factors as well. For example, discounters base their fees on the *number* of shares traded, the *dollar value* of the transaction, or a *combination* of both. In general, the larger the number of shares being bought or sold, or the higher the dollar value of the trade, the larger the client's savings on commission. Most discounters impose minimum commissions to ensure that their rates exceed those of full-service brokerage firms on small trades.

Some discount brokerage firms charge larger commissions than their contemporaries because of the additional kinds of service provided to clients. For example, many discount brokers accept orders anytime during the day or night by telephone with toll-free numbers, even though those orders are actually executed the next day when the stock exchange is open. In general, service (i.e., trading execution) among discount brokers is the same, but pricing schedules vary. Before you open an account with a discount broker, shop around and compare charges of different discount brokers on the types of trades you expect to make, since lower prices are the main incentive for using a discounter. Referrals from friends or professional colleagues is advisable.

Consider a full-service broker if you would feel more comfortable with professional advice about buy and sell decisions, and if you recognize your limitations in studying and interpreting the complexities of the stock market. Also, a full-service broker generally will be available to answer questions when the need arises and keeps you informed on new stock offerings. Full-service brokerage firms also provide a variety of investment packages that might fit within your investment objectives, such as unit investment trusts, municipal bonds, limited partnerships, life insurance, and annuities.

Another consideration for using a full-service broker is the price and quantity of the shares you buy and sell. For example, if you trade in odd lots of stock (i.e., fewer than 100 shares) you are probably better off with a full-service broker than a discount broker. A full-service broker will charge about the same as a discounter for executing odd-lot transactions.

If you are a long-term investor who studies the market, follows industry trends, and looks for stocks of companies with a high potential for success, you are probably better off dealing with a discount broker. Also, if you are not an active investor at present and want to sell stocks you received as a gift, inheritance, or as part of a company benefits plan, a discount broker should be used to execute the trade. Further, if you engage in simple transactions, such as buying and selling blue-chip stocks, you might also consider using a discount broker.

Many people use a full-service broker on some trades, such as investments with above-average risks, and a discount broker on others. But only use a discount broker on trades where you feel comfortable with your own buy and sell investment decisions.

Most people become too emotional about the stock market, and have little time to devote to monitoring its complex gyrations in a bull and bear market climate. In order to make a prudent decision on buying and selling securities, you need the right temperament, time, talent, and information. Most of us do not have some or all of these qualities for developing a long-term investment plan. In these instances, the services of a full-service broker are probably the practical approach to consider.

A full-service broker is able to tell you when to buy or sell a particular investment, and also keeps you informed as to what is going on in the securities market. For example, the president of a high-tech company in California earned a great deal of money over a three-year period as a result of his relationship with a full-service stockbroker who instructed the president when to buy and sell certain stocks at the appropriate time.

For complex deals that require close monitoring and guidance to fulfill investment objectives, such as when buying and selling stock options, use a full-service broker. For simple transactions, like trading blue-chip stocks, use a discount broker. An owner of a retail outlet in New York City splits his accounts between both types of brokers. A full-service broker is used for investments in mortgage-backed securities that require specialized investment knowledge. The businessperson uses a discount broker for investments in blue-chip stocks, such as General Motors, the activity of which can be easily followed in financial reports and in newspapers such as *The Wall Street Journal*.

Always compare the fees of several brokers in each class,

because fees are affected by several factors, particularly the number of shares and the amount of money involved. Some brokers have low rates but require large minimums that make it costly for small trades. In any event, both full-service and discount brokers generally give better rates to their more active customers.

Charges for services by discount brokers may vary widely. For example, Mercer, Inc., a New York City financial publisher, conducted its seventh "Discount Brokerage Survey," the results of which were in the June 1990 issue of *Money* magazine. The survey queried 175 discount brokerage firms as to what they would charge for 25 different trades. The least expensive firm charged $22.99 for a trade of 100 shares at $50 each, while three prominent and larger discount brokerage firms charged $48.00, $46.33, and $49.00, respectively, for the same type of transaction.

38

SEARCHING FOR
THE RIGHT BROKER

Selecting brokerage services is a highly personal decision. Care and diligence should be employed in your search for the right stockbroker, because the quality of service you receive will depend on the brokerage firm and sales representative or stockbroker you choose.

Ask your friends and business associates who are successful investors for recommendations. However, remember that these individuals may have financial situations, needs, objectives, temperaments, and investment philosophies that differ from yours. Try to get referrals from those with financial situations and investment goals similar to your own. You could also get referrals from your lawyer, certified public accountant, banker, or other professionals you trust.

Another way to search for a good stockbroker is through investment seminars, which are periodically advertised in local newspapers. Such seminars are often conducted by a broker from a reputable firm, and may cover a variety of subjects relating to retirement planning, setting up a trust fund, planning for a child's education, and other investment-related topics. Look for a seminar that covers a subject that is compatible with your investment interests and goals.

If you decide to attend an investment seminar, evaluate the broker and his or her presentation. If you like the broker's overall demeanor and approach, make an effort to introduce yourself after the presentation, and ask any questions regarding your investment goals or situation. If you are pleased with the broker's answers, arrange for a personal interview at the brokerage firm's office.

After you have made a decision to meet one or several brokers, you might request from each prospect the following information on the broker's firm: a brochure that describes the investment products offered by the firm, a list of services provided by the firm, a list of specific recommendations made to investors by the firm over the past few years, and a copy of the firm's commission rates. A study of these items should enable you to address specific questions to the broker at your initial meeting.

The initial meeting with a stockbroker should be regarded as an interview. Discuss your investment objectives and financial capabilities openly. Facts provided to the broker will enable him or her to advise you properly and to develop a program that is suited to your particular situation.

During the initial interview, do not hesitate to ask questions. Remember, there is no such thing as a dumb question, especially when your investment dollars are involved. Listen carefully to the answers you receive, and note the prospective broker's personal style and manner. Does he or she appear to be pushy or low-key? Are answers to the questions in plain English or weighted down with Wall Street jargon? Does the broker make reference only to those investment products carried by his or her firm?

Questions addressed to a prospective broker should relate to the following:

- The size of the portfolios managed by the broker.
- Number of years of experience the broker has in the market.
- Industry groups the broker believes to have the most potential in the immediate as well as long-term future.
- Risk factors associated with the broker's recommendations.

If the stockbroker is young and perhaps not as experienced as other candidates interviewed, concentrate on the broker's interest in the market and his or her current knowledge. A broker new on the scene may not possess the "market sense" of his or her more experienced contemporaries, but may have recent training in the newer packaged investments, such as limited partnerships and mutual funds. Brokers just starting out often work harder for their clients in order to build up their client base through possible referrals. Since they are fresh out of training, most new brokers follow their respective firm's research carefully and sell the latest packaged

102

investment products. If a broker has at least three to five years' experience, he or she is probably well-qualified to handle your account and is in the business to stay. A brokerage firm in St. Louis, Missouri, hires ten potential brokers for every one hundred candidates interviewed. During the first year of work, seven out of ten remain with the firm. Five brokers survive the second year, and four of the brokers remain in the firm by the fourth year.

An experienced broker with several years in the business who has many accounts may not be for you, especially if your account begins with a modest-sized investment. Most experienced brokers direct their energies to servicing the large portfolios that generate the most commissions.

When you have narrowed your search to one or two stockbrokers, it may be a prudent exercise to double-check their backgrounds. The National Association of Securities Dealers (NASD), the self-regulatory group for the OTC market, can provide such assistance. The NASD provides an "Information Request Form," which can be obtained by writing to the NASD Membership Department, P.O. Box 9401, Gaithersburg, Maryland 20898, or telephone its information services line at (301) 738-6500 and request a copy of the form. Submit the filled-out form to the NASD and the organization will send you back a summary of the education, employment history, and any criminal or disciplinary record of the NASD's registered stockbrokers. If requested, the NASD will also list any infractions committed by the broker's firm. In some cases, you may have to pay a nominal processing fee for this information.

State securities administrators can provide a similar background check on brokers or firms conducting business within their state. You can obtain the state administrator's telephone number by calling the North American Securities Administrators Association at (800) 942-9022. Also, write to the Securities and Exchange Commission's Freedom of Information Branch, 450 Fifth Street, N.W., Mail Stop 2-6, Washington, D.C. 20549, for any federal records of complaints against stockbrokers or brokerage firms.

As an individual, you cannot buy and sell securities by yourself. Transactions must be executed by a stockbroker, who is a registered representative of a stock exchange. Stockbrokers must pass a difficult and exacting written examination and a rigorous training program in preparation for licensing requirements.

In order to be licensed by the SEC as a registered representative on behalf of a brokerage firm, a broker-dealer trainee must pass a Series 7 examination, which leads to the designation "general securities registered representative." The exam encompasses several areas relating to the securities industry, such as corporate equity and debt securities, U.S. government bonds, municipal bonds, financial statement analysis, NYSE administrative/exchange transactions, OTC transactions, opening and handling brokerage accounts, processing orders, and stock exchange rules and regulations. Brokers may also take other securities licensing examinations that qualify them as specialists in certain areas. For example, passing the Series 3 examination qualifies a commodity futures representative to sell all types of commodities and futures, which include agriculture, interest rate, foreign currency, and stock indexes. Successful completion of the Series 6 examination earns a broker the title "investment company/variable contracts representative" and qualifies him or her to sell mutual funds, variable annuities, and profit-sharing and tax-deferred annuity plans.

The most important consideration in selecting a stockbroker and a brokerage firm is that the firm's products, services, recommendations, and commission structure are comparable with your investment goals and objectives. You must feel confident that the particular stockbroker you have chosen understands your objectives and can help you to achieve them.

39

OPENING AN ACCOUNT WITH A BROKER

When you decide to engage a particular stockbroker, you will assist him or her in filling out a new account form. This form is necessary to establish certain facts about you as a customer. For example, you will need to answer questions concerning your net worth, annual income, investment objectives, risk tolerance, income-tax bracket, and current employment. Questions on these matters should not be construed as an intrusion on your privacy. The more a stockbroker knows about you, the better he or she can service you and help you make the proper investment decisions to meet your needs and objectives. All the information you disclose to a broker is kept confidential.

You must complete additional forms if you decide to open a *margin account*. A margin account is a credit arrangement that enables you, as an investor, to use your securities as collateral to buy more securities. A brokerage firm lends you part of the purchase price of the securities. In a bear market, margin accounts tend to create a domino effect. For example, when stocks drop in value, margin investors have two options: 1) put up more collateral (i.e., more stock), or; 2) liquidate some of their holdings.

If investors decide to sell their stocks, the stock's price is driven further down. This, in turn, forces other margin investors into a similar position (i.e., selling out stock holdings), and the stock price is driven down even further. A momentum builds up from this downward cycle that becomes difficult to reverse. A prime example was the stock-market crash of 1929 and, to a certain extent, the crash of 1987.

You as an investor may open a *discretionary account*, in which you give the broker complete authority to make all your buy and sell decisions without first consulting you.

Discretionary accounts are also used by money managers (See Keys 27 to 34) and are appropriate for blind trusts rather than for active investors. Some brokerage firms refuse to accept discretionary power over an account or limit such accounts to their most seasoned senior brokers. Discretionary accounts are open to abuse by people who receive commissions based on the number of transactions in the account.

For example, a stockbroker from a brokerage firm in Minneapolis, Minnesota, does not like to have full discretionary authority over an account because she regards such authority as a *fiduciary responsibility* that she feels to be unethical when a broker is compensated by commissions on buy and sell transactions. On the other hand, an experienced broker from a national firm in New York City has discretionary authority over approximately one thousand accounts, and has averaged almost a 20-percent annual rate of return including compounding for those clients over the last 10 years. However, this is an exception, since the firm generally discourages discretionary accounts.

Do not open a margin or discretionary account unless you clearly understand how these accounts operate and appreciate the risks associated with them. As a beginning investor, you are better off without a margin or discretionary account until you become more savvy and knowledgeable.

40

THE CLIENT-BROKER RELATIONSHIP

In order to maintain a profitable and satisfactory relationship with your stockbroker, communication is essential. In general, the frequency of contact should be consistent with your investment objectives and the size of your portfolio.

If your account comprises five to 10 different stocks for purposes of long-term conservative growth, you can probably limit broker contact to once or twice a year. On the other hand, if your portfolio includes 20 to 30 growth or speculative stocks, the account requires closer supervision and a broker might need to call you several times a week.

Regardless of the size of your portfolio, you might ask your broker to call you on a periodic basis, such as once a month, so you both can discuss maintenance control of your account. In any event, use your discretion as to the frequency of contact with your broker. There is no set rule that applies to every type of account.

To be a prudent investor, you need to be informed. Make an effort to understand each of your investments. This includes:

- How it is structured,
- Inherent benefits and risks, and
- Whether it is in line with your investment strategy.

Your best information source is the stockbroker who services your account. The broker should periodically provide you with the publications available from the firm's research department that enable you to keep current on market trends, investment possibilities, and other relevant financial information.

As an investor in a particular company, you are an owner of that enterprise. You should know as much as possible about the company, such as the current share price and any other

107

developments relative to its market performance. Ask your broker for quarterly and annual reports about the companies with which you are interested. Such reports provide invaluable information on current earnings, cash-flow position, a view of past performance and future prospects, discussions of new products, the status of labor relations, and the company's social responsibility (e.g., impact of products on the environment).

On a periodic basis, usually quarterly, the brokerage firm mails you a complete statement of your account that shows your investment holdings and any activity that has taken place since the prior statement, including interest and dividend payments and buy and sell orders. These statements should be kept on file, both to keep you up-to-date on your account and for tax-return information. If there is any item on the statement that you do not understand, call your broker for clarification.

When your broker recommends an investment, he or she should educate you on the recommended stocks. If the broker urges you to buy a number of shares of stock in a particular company, pose a question, such as "What else is your firm recommending that fits my investment objectives?". The broker might be under pressure from the firm to push the sale of stocks of that particular company. This type of question forces the broker to propose investment alternatives for you.

A small brokerage firm in California pressured its brokers to sell a speculative stock that appeared to have growth potential. The firm's research director felt that the stock was overpriced, but the brokers continued to sell the stock to their clients, which drove the stock's price upward. During a six-month period, the stock price rose from 1¼ to 3¼ per share. When the firm had sold 543,000 shares of the stock to over 1,000 investors, an investigation was undertaken by the National Association of Securities Dealers (NASD). As a result of the investigation, the firm was charged with several violations of SEC rules, including manipulation and high-pressure sales tactics.

Stockbrokers are salespeople. Make sure that they are knowledgeable about their recommendations. If a broker recommends a particular stock, ask the following questions:

• Has your firm or a security analyst researched this com-

pany?
- Do you consider the stock undervalued?
- What is the rate of earnings growth that I might expect from this stock?
- What information do you have to indicate that the company is well-managed?
- What reasons can you give me for buying this stock now rather than at some future time?
- How does this stock fit into my investment objectives?
- Are there any large shareholders in the company?
- Is there any chance that the stock value will decrease rather than rise in light of the current economic climate?
- What exchange trades the company's shares?

In order to ensure a mutually beneficial relationship between you and your broker, use common courtesy. This can be accomplished as follows:

- Be honest regarding your investment objectives and how much money you have to invest.
- Return telephone calls promptly to your broker, since time is of the essence for proper market timing.
- Follow the broker's advice if you feel comfortable with his or her recommendations.
- Set realistic expectations for your investments.
- Provide your broker with all relevant information you hear about the companies in which you are investing so that he or she can analyze it with respect to your investment objectives.
- Provide referrals of potential clients to your broker.
- Never call your broker on a daily basis for stock quotes.

Courteous dealings with your stockbroker will enhance your position as a valued customer or client. For example, a broker with a national firm in New York City received several referrals from a client, including the client's parents, brother, boss, and two co-workers. As a result, the broker informs the client, almost on a weekly basis, about any developments on present stock holdings as well as potential investment packages.

41

AVOIDING INVESTMENT PITFALLS

"Caveat emptor" (Let the buyer beware), an adage that dates back to the Roman Empire, is an admonition that still holds true, especially when it comes to investing money. When implementing your investment goals, "caveat emptor" means never be taken in by false promises or "get-rich-quick" schemes. In the long run, such hopes are never fulfilled, and the hopeful investors always become the hopeless.

Approach your investment goals prudently. Avoid stocks or bonds that are solicited over the telephone, regardless of how persuasive the person on the other end sounds and regardless of how many promises he or she makes. This type of selling by telephone is done by "con men," not by reputable stock-brokers.

Selling by telephone is often referred to on Wall Street as "cold calling." The typical "boiler-room operation" contains rows of desks with only telephones on them. Assigned to each of the phones is a salesperson who sells securities and asks that payment be sent to a post office box number. In most cases, the securities are either highly speculative or worthless. The boiler-room operation eventually closes up shop and disappears with the cash of all its unwitting "investors."

This writer has encountered salesmen from boiler-room operations on a few occasions. For example, one afternoon I received a telephone call at my office from a man with a resonant and vibrant voice who introduced himself as a representative of an investment advisory firm. He asked me if I was actively involved in investing in the stock market, to which I replied "yes." He proceeded to tell me that he had a unique investment opportunity for me to consider. I asked him how he got my office telephone number, after which he abruptly hung up. Some of my associates in the office had received similar telephone calls that week. I could only assume that the boiler-room operators somehow obtained copies of the company's interoffice telephone directory.

Another investment pitfall to avoid are mailings that offer bargain stocks that you receive for sending money to the mailer, which again is usually a post office box number. Every year millions of dollars are lost by naive investors through such mail-fraud operations.

Never purchase securities on the basis of "tips" or "rumors" regardless of who provides you with the information. If all so-called "hot" tips were legitimate, we would be a nation of millionaires. Keep your eyes and ears open and base investment decisions on fact rather than emotion. A reputable stockbroker encourages you to buy securities with potential value based on factual data and reliable information and won't mind if you ask a lot of questions.

If you are a new investor, avoid securities that are initial public offerings, since they are usually *unseasoned stocks* of companies offering their securities for the first time. In many cases, securities of these companies are sold "over-the-counter." Information about these companies is generally hard to obtain, because unlisted companies are not required to publish earnings, sales, income, or any other information that can be used as a basis for arriving at an investment decision.

Focus your attention on listed companies—that is, companies whose stocks are listed on the New York Stock Exchange, the American Stock Exchange, or other regional stock exchanges. Listed securities have certain advantages over unlisted securities, such as financial strength, readily available information on the companies, and a large pool of shareholders, which makes it easier to sell the securities.

In general, investment pitfalls can be minimized by adhering to certain rules:

- Never transact business via telephone solicitations from strangers.
- Ignore "get-rich-quick" schemes that promise immediate fortunes.
- Never be coaxed by high-pressure sales talks.
- Never purchase stocks and bonds based on "hot" tips or rumors; rather, obtain some documented information on

investment opportunities (e.g., a prospectus, annual report, etc.).
- Avoid speculating in the stock market.
- Never invest beyond your financial means.

The majority of stockbrokers are honest, reputable, and trustworthy. However, there are some that are motivated by greed and may take dangerous risks with your money.

The following are some unethical ploys:

Misrepresentation—Stockbrokers are similar to salesmen in that they try to convince you to buy a stock their firm recommends. In general, you should seriously consider your broker's recommendations. However, be wary of the exaggerated sales pitches, such as "I guarantee that the selling price of this stock should double within the next year or two." Any form of guarantee by a broker as to the future performance of a particular stock is a violation of securities laws.

Another inducement often used by a broker is when he or she states that the price of a stock will double based on "good authority." If such a statement is true, the broker may be in violation of laws relating to insider information. Your investment decisions should be based on facts and information obtained from the brokerage firm's research department and not from exaggerated statements of potential wealth.

Inadequate recommendations—An unethical broker will often recommend investments that do not fit into your overall investment plan. For example, a logical investment objective for an elderly person would be to invest life savings in conservative investments that would generate a steady flow of annual income, preferably tax fee. An overly aggressive broker might recommend speculative stocks to be purchased on margin. In this way, the account would be handled on an active basis, and the broker would generate a continual stream of commissions.

An elderly widow from Rochester, New York, allocated most of her $115,000 life savings to a new account with a stockbroker. In light of her age, she needed investment income. Instead of buying conservative, income-generating investments, the broker recommended options and speculative stocks purchased on margin. Within one year, the broker earned $25,000 in commissions as a result of executing over

130 transactions. She finally referred the situation to the NASD after receiving a margin call for $80,000 for a speculative gold mining stock recommended by the broker. As a result of the broker's actions, he was charged with unsuitable recommendations and excessive trading, fined $10,000, and suspended from serving as a NASD registered representative for a period of time.

A broker should *never* recommend any investments that are riskier than the client is able to handle.

Churning—Excessive trading in your account may be undertaken by a broker in order to earn commissions. In this way, the broker "churns" or rotates a client's account so that investments are continually bought and sold within a short period of days or hours. Unless you are an active trader who is interested in speculating, or you have a discretionary account where the broker is granted the authority to make buy and sell decisions on your behalf, your account should *not* be subject to churning.

A case was reported by the NASD where a broker interposed his wife's account with that of his clients. For instance, when a client placed an order, the broker would fill the order by selling shares short in his wife's account and then buying those shares for a client. After the transaction was completed, the broker would purchase more shares for his wife's account in order to cover her short position. Those shares would always be purchased at a price that was lower than the price of the stock charged to the client. An SEC investigation revealed that the broker was making a double profit on each transaction, that is, a profit on the stock for his wife and a commission from the client.

Unauthorized trades—Some brokers may buy and sell securities without your permission. This practice often occurs when you might be on an extended vacation, and the broker claims that you were not reachable at the time this great investment opportunity arose. Again, unless you have a discretionary account, do not allow your broker to buy and sell securities for you without your permission. Unauthorized trades generally start on a small scale and eventually have a snowball effect.

Misappropriation of funds—An unethical broker may steal

113

money from clients by tampering with their accounts. For example, funds from client A's account may be diverted to client B's account, and then later moved back to client A's account. This illegal practice is often difficult to detect. Scrutinize your monthly statement for current activity that was authorized by your instructions.

Unethical ploys, such as misrepresentation, inadequate recommendations, churning, unauthorized trades, and misappropriation of funds do not emerge as a result of one single act by a stockbroker. They usually result from a series of repeated actions that begin on a small scale. After a period of time, a pattern of increasing abuse evolves which may affect several investors. If you recognize *any* of these unethical ploys, inform your brokerage firm immediately. Most brokerage firms will respond to your allegations promptly in order to avoid any potential legal problems.

42

EVALUATING STOCKBROKER PERFORMANCE

Evaluate your stockbroker's performance annually to determine whether to continue the business relationship or find another broker. Trust might be the most important criterion for evaluation. You should feel that the broker has concern for your interests. A stockbroker with a national brokerage firm in Los Angeles, California, encourages new clients to call him when they receive their first monthly statement so that he can guide them through it and explain the various code words and abbreviations. Ask your broker to explain anything you do not understand on the monthly statement. Find out whether the firm provides a brochure or booklet on how to read the monthly brokerage statement. Some firms provide this service as an accommodation to customers.

You must feel confident that your broker is concerned about your account, and that he or she will not mislead you into making any unsound investment decisions. For example, has your broker talked you *out* of a transaction when you wanted to sell a stock that appeared to be going down in value, or when you wanted to buy a stock that appeared to have growth potential? If, some time later, you discovered that the broker made a prudent decision by recommending that you not sell or buy a stock, this is a sign of a trustworthy broker. He or she forfeited a commission in order to keep you from making unnecessary transactions.

Another criterion of trust is whether your broker provides you with a straightforward assessment of a situation when a recommended investment fails to materialize. For example, a sincere broker will admit making a bad judgment call. A trustworthy broker will discourage you from investments that appear questionable, such as bonds with a risk that is too high for your investment philosophy.

Another important consideration is the quality of service. For example, adequate service from a stockbroker should include the following:

- Information on new investment opportunities (e.g., research reports).
- Resolution of any problems with your account and timely answers to questions.
- Telephone calls to inform you about buying or selling a particular stock and the price of your executed trades.
- Annual reviews of your portfolio.

Stockbrokers should also be evaluated on their investment knowledge. Through periodic contacts with your broker, determine whether he or she is vigilant about following the daily movement of the stock market, and whether the broker provides an opinion on the future direction of the market.

An annual review of your portfolio should provide you with the results of your stockbroker's efforts in helping you to achieve your investment goals. Determine the total value of your investments in conjunction with the money you received in income and/or sales of stocks and bonds, and subtract the total amount of money invested with your broker. The difference is the amount of money your broker has earned or lost for your account. After you calculate your profit, determine whether or not you have achieved your investment objective, such as realizing a certain percentage of tax-free income. If you feel that you may have done better with a bank certificate of deposit or a money-market account, it may be time to find another stockbroker.

Finally, determine whether your broker shows understanding—that is, whether the broker listens to your concerns and takes the necessary time to service your investment needs in light of your objectives and assumable risk. For example, a vice president of a small manufacturing company in Pennsylvania has been a longtime client of a broker affiliated with the Philadelphia office of a national brokerage firm. Although the officer of the company likes to pick and choose her own stocks as a "hobby," the broker discusses her selections, researches them, and provides his views as to whether her selections show any promise.

Understanding between you and your broker also entails compatibility. You should feel comfortable when dealing with your broker. Does he or she level with you in conversations, or talk over your head as though trying to impress you? There should be a rapport between you and your stockbroker. If you do not feel comfortable with the broker and lack confidence in the relationship, look for another stockbroker.

When evaluating your stockbroker, consider the additional small courtesies paid to you as a client, such as sending you copies of articles relating to the companies in which you own stock, or perhaps giving you some leeway on commissions for certain trades. For example, a broker in Minneapolis, Minnesota makes it a practice to liquidate his client's position in a stock that does poorly, which he previously recommended. This is done without a charge to the client. By not charging a commission, the broker feels that the gesture is his way of apologizing for recommending an investment that did not pan out. Two partners from a New York City brokerage firm will provide an "extra" for their clients by sponsoring seminars, including meals and an open bar, that inform their clients of timely information on new investments.

43

INFORMATION SOURCES ON YOUR PORTFOLIO

Even if your stockbroker is capable of guiding your portfolio to profit, and his or her performance appears to be on target, do some monitoring on your own. A wise investor is an informed investor. Your hard-earned investment dollars are on the line, and you need to know as much as you can about the securities you invest in. By keeping tabs on those companies, you generate intelligent questions for your broker about your portfolio. In addition to commanding respect from your broker, you keep him on his toes.

You do not have to be a financial analyst to monitor the performance of your securities. Refer to sources of information on those companies, such as the following:

- *Financial reports*—You can find valuable information about companies from their annual reports, which can be obtained directly from those companies or from your broker. Quarterly or interim financial information is also generally available on companies that issue annual reports. Financial reports contain a statement of the company's earnings, its views on past performance and future prospects, discussions of new products and services, and the impact of the environment on the company's present and future position. (To obtain practical explanations of the vital aspects of annual reports, see *Keys to Reading An Annual Report*, also published by Barron's Educational Series.)
- *Financial news*—Many newspapers, such as *The Wall Street Journal*, provide daily information on listed companies and the stock market. The business or financial sections of these daily papers include stock tables that

report daily price changes and other information, including yields, price earnings ratios, and other relevant data about stocks listed on major exchanges and over-the-counter (OTC) markets. (For further information on this topic, refer to *Keys to Understanding the Financial News*, also published by Barron's.) These newspapers also report news about the corporate and financial world that may be relevant to your investments.

- *Business periodicals and newsletters*—There are numerous business periodicals and newsletters to which you may subscribe or that are available from your local library, which contain information on companies, recommended stocks, trends in different industries, the stock market in general, and the impact of the economy on certain industries and the stock market. Periodicals include *Money* magazine and Kiplinger's *Personal Finance* magazine. There are newsletters that analyze individual stocks and provide weekly reports on stock activity, such as the *Value Line Investment Survey*, *Market Logic*, and *Growth Stock Outlook*. Subscriptions to such newsletters are generally expensive, so your best bet is to review them at a local business library.

44

CONTROLLING YOUR STOCKBROKER

If you have any problems with your stockbroker or believe that your account is not being properly handled, discuss the situation with your stockbroker. If necessary, discuss it further with your broker's branch manager. Call either or both parties and follow up with a letter stating your complaint and describing the circumstances surrounding the situation.

You may also wish to send a formal letter of complaint to the chief compliance officer of the brokerage firm. The compliance officer's address should be obtainable from your broker, the firm's office manager, or your state securities commission.

If you do not receive a satisfactory response from any of these sources, several agencies can mediate your dispute. File a formal written complaint with any of the following: The Securities and Exchange Commission (SEC), National Association of Securities Dealers (NASD), the Municipal Securities Rulemaking Board (MSRB), the New York Stock Exchange (NYSE), the American Stock Exchange (AMEX), or other securities exchanges. In order to avoid duplication of effort, write to only one of these organizations, preferably the one that has jurisdiction over the dispute.

The Securities and Exchange Commission. The SEC oversees and regulates the securities industry and is empowered to do the following:

1. Register new securities and mutual funds.
2. Ensure that investors obtain accurate information from corporations.
3. Monitor securities markets to ensure fair and orderly conduct.
4. Oversee the securities industry's self-regulating organizations (SROs), such as the NYSE and the NASD.

As an oversight body, the SEC can offer limited help with grievances. The SEC acts as a neutral third party and mediates disputes. The SEC cannot arbitrate a dispute, but will refer you to the appropriate SRO arbitration program.

The SEC can inform you as to whether a brokerage firm is registered, and the number of complaints that have been brought against the firm. Information on investigations and litigation under the Freedom of Information Act (FOIA) can be obtained by writing to the FOIA officer at the SEC office in Washington, D.C. Contact the SEC at the following address:

The Securities and Exchange Commission
Office of Consumer Affairs and Information Services
450 Fifth Avenue, N.W.
Washington, D.C. 20549
(202) 272-7440

The SEC also has regional and branch offices that handle complaints. It might be more convenient to submit a complaint to the SEC regional office instead of the Washington, D.C., office. Call the national office in Washington, D.C., to obtain the regional office that is located in your vicinity.

National Association of Securities Dealers. The NASD is a self-regulatory agency of the over-the-counter securities industry, and possesses the power to fine, suspend, or bar a member firm from securities trading. In order to recover money, the NASD Arbitration Division operates one of the most frequently used programs. This SRO can be contacted at:

National Association of Securities Dealers
1735 K Street, N.W.
Washington, D.C. 20006
(202) 728-8000

To proceed with an arbitration claim, contact:

National Association of Securities Dealers Arbitration Division
Two World Trade Center
New York, New York 10048
(212) 839-6251

The Municipal Securities Rulemaking Board. The MSRB regulates the underwriting, trading, and selling of *municipal* securities. The MSRB arbitrates claims, and its decisions are final. The Board can be contacted at:

The Municipal Securities Rulemaking Board Arbitration
Case Administrator
1818 N Street, N.W.
Washington, D.C. 20036
(202) 223-9347

Stock Exchanges. Various stock exchanges, such as the New York Stock Exchange and the American Stock Exchange, are also SROs and will mediate your claim. If mediation fails, they will arbitrate.

Most client-stockbroker disputes can be resolved through *arbitration*, a mechanism established by the securities industry to expedite disputes. The SEC and other SROs described in this chapter provide brochures on arbitration that detail how to proceed with an arbitration claim; the brochures can be obtained by writing or calling these agencies. In general, arbitration is a method whereby a dispute between two or more parties is resolved by impartial persons who are knowledgeable in the controversial area.

Disputed claims with stockbrokers can also be reported to the Securities Investor Protection Corporation (SIPC), 805 Fifteenth Street, N.W., Washington, D.C. 20005-2207. (For a description of SIPC, see Key 36.)

A dispute with your stockbroker can also be pursued in court. However, legal action should be considered only if the case involves a substantial amount of money, because hourly legal fees are high. If you decide on litigation, obtain an attorney who has experience in securities-law cases. Arbitration through the NASD or through a recognized stock exchange should be the initial approach in handling a dispute before taking legal action. It is less costly and generally a faster means of resolving a claim as compared to litigation.

For example, a Florida doctor sued his brokerage firm because a $150,000 tax-shelter investment did not meet his expectations. After four years of pretrial claims, the case went to trial, and the jury ruled against the doctor on every claim. The doctor's legal fees amounted to $100,000, and he was also liable for the legal fees of the brokerage firm. A similar situation, also in Florida, involved a blind paraplegic who lost legal suit against his broker and became liable for the broker's legal fees.

These two incidents show that one should carefully consider whether litigating a securities case would be worthwhile.

In addition to situations regarding disputes which might ultimately lead to arbitration, you should consider changing your broker whenever any of the following occur:

- Your broker avoids calling you when the value of your investments continue to scale downward.
- Your investment objectives are not on target, and accordingly the return on your investments does not appear to be meeting your expectations.
- There is a breakdown in communications between you and your broker as exemplified by the broker not returning phone calls, being unable to provide direct answers to your questions, or failing to follow your instructions.
- Your broker tends to switch brokerage firms too frequently, and accordingly moves your account to another firm that may not have an investment philosophy which coincides with yours.
- Your broker has a tendency to pressure you into buying investments that do not fit your goals.

If you should encounter any one or more of these situations, consider firing your broker and changing to someone else.

A widow in her seventies had a portfolio that consisted of government backed securities and conservative utility stocks in order to meet her investment objectives of safety and income. Her broker encouraged her to purchase more aggressive investments. She followed his advice and bought some shares in a speculative stock. He continued to be more aggressive in getting her to buy more of the speculative stock.

Finally, without her consent, he bought several thousand shares of the speculative stock which eventually declined in price. As a result, the widow's portfolio fell in value.

The broker's insistence on an aggressive strategy for a conservative investor led to loss of a client, and to an indictment for violating SEC regulations as a result of investing funds without a client's approval.

45

THE EXCHANGE COMMUNITY

When dealing with stockbrokers, you should have some familiarity with the exchange community, which encompasses numerous stock exchanges throughout the United States. A stock exchange can be described as a meeting place where people buy and sell stocks, bonds, and other investment certificates. It is analogous to a huge marketplace where all types of goods are bought and sold.

In general, the stock exchange brings buyers and sellers together. It is these buyers and sellers who determine the price of the stock. If a corporation increases earnings in the current year over the prior year, the potential of the stock becomes favorable. The demand for the stock increases, which may lead to an increase in the stock price. As the price increases, more stock is offered by stockholders for sale to the public. If more stock is offered for sale than can be bought at a given time, the price of the stock will level off or may decline.

Stockbrokers acts as *agents* for the buyers and sellers of stocks, bonds, and other investment certificates. They *bid* a price for a customer when he or she wants to buy a security and offer to sell the security at a certain price. In between the bid and offer price, a stock will be bought and sold. The matching of a bid and offer price is referred to as a *trade*.

The largest stock exchange in the United States is the New York Stock Exchange (NYSE), located at 11 Wall Street in New York City. Often referred to as the Big Board, the NYSE lists some of the largest well-capitalized companies in the world. The NYSE is known for blue-chip stocks that have demonstrated their ability to pay dividends to stockholders during good and bad market cycles.

The National Association of Securities Dealers (NASD) is the second-largest stock exchange and SRO in the United

States. The NASD lists the shares of growth-oriented companies that are usually not as large or as seasoned as NYSE-listed companies.

There are other stock exchanges, such as the American Stock Exchange, that also market the stocks of large corporations, and other regional exchanges also trade companies already listed on the New York and American stock exchanges, such as the Boston Stock Exchange, the Pacific Stock Exchange, the Philadelphia Stock Exchange, and the Midwest Stock Exchange. This duplication of listed companies can be useful to investors who want to get the best price when they transact buy and sell orders or do business after the NYSE and AMEX close. The Pacific Stock Exchange closes after the closing of the NYSE and AMEX. If any new developments occur, investors are still able to buy and sell. For example, on November 22, 1963, the day President John F. Kennedy was assassinated, trading volume was heavy on the Pacific Stock Exchange well after the close of the NYSE.

Most brokerage firms are members of many stock exchanges. To become a member of an exchange, the firm must meet certain requirements. For example, a NYSE member firm is required to do the following:

- Furnish customers with the firm's most recent financial statements upon request.
- Maintain specified capital levels at all times.
- Pass annual audits and be prepared for periodic audit checks by NYSE examiners.
- File several financial reports with the NYSE, which includes the report based on the annual audit.
- Disclose to the NYSE details concerning certain borrowings or loans by the brokerage firm or by individual firm partners.
- Carry fidelity insurance coverage for all firm employees and principals.

Also, in order for a stockbrokerage to be a member of the NYSE, at least one member of the firm must own a seat on the exchange. Both stockbrokers and their brokerage firm are required to adhere to these requirements, which also include a lengthy book of NYSE rules and regulations that serves as a code of ethics.

Many brokerage firms are also members of the National Association of Securities Dealers (NASD). NASD membership enables brokers and dealers to trade stocks over-the-counter and act as dealers or market makers in those stocks. For example, more than 4,200 companies list their securities on NASDAQ, the National Association of Securities Dealers Automated Quotations, which is more than the number of companies listed with NYSE and AMEX combined. Companies whose stocks trade OTC include Apple and MCI. Unlike listed securities that have bidding by stockbrokers on an exchange floor, an over-the-counter stock is bought and sold strictly by trading carried on "upstairs" by brokers and dealers over telephones. There is no physical contact between buying and selling brokers; transactions are automatically executed via computer. This ensures a speedy, efficient transaction in an effort to guarantee the client the best price. In general, some NASDAQ stocks are considered to be more speculative than most NYSE and AMEX stocks.

In addition to being members of a recognized stock exchange, some brokerage firms may be members of a trade association, such as the Securities Industry Association (SIA). The SIA represents over 600 securities firms located throughout the United States and Canada, members of which include investment bankers, brokers, dealers, and mutual-fund companies. An SIA member firm must have a net worth of at least $50,000. The Association provides the following for its members:

- Serves as a forum for addressing issues that affect the securities industry.
- Acts as a conduit for information and ideas on securities management and regulation.
- Provides a center for securities-industry studies.
- Offers various services to assist officials of member firms in their management responsibilities, which includes educational conferences and programs.

QUESTIONS AND ANSWERS

What kinds of services do CPAs perform for their clients?

CPAs provide a variety of services that relate to financial statements, accounting and bookkeeping, taxation, management consulting, and financial planning.

How does a certified public accountant differ from a non-CPA accountant?

A CPA is someone who meets certain statutory requirements in order to become licensed by a state or territory. Those requirements relate to college-level education, passing a uniform statewide examination, and working as an accountant for a public accounting firm for a specified period of time.

What is the most important factor to consider in selecting a CPA?

A CPA must possess the necessary technical competence to service your needs. For example, if you have a business, the CPA should be familiar with that business and any specific accounting and financial reporting matters relating to the industry of which the business is a part. Also, if you hire a CPA to prepare an income-tax return, determine whether the CPA can engage in tax consulting and tax-compliance matters.

Are CPAs subject to any rules and standards?

In practicing public accounting, CPAs are governed by various rules and standards promulgated by the state board of accountancy that grants them a CPA certificate. Professional organizations, such as the American Institute of Certified Public Accountants and state societies of CPAs, design standards for CPAs to follow in order to adequately serve the public interest.

When would it be worthwhile to use a financial planner?

Since financial planners generally charge from $250 to $2,500 or more for a financial plan, they should only be engaged if you have savings of approximately $20,000 or more. If you have less than $20,000 to invest, consider high-yield certificates of deposit, money-market funds, and/or mutual funds.

Is there any way to determine the professional competence of a financial planner?

Qualified financial planners should possess one or more designations or titles to indicate appropriate training and experience, such as certified financial planner (CFP), chartered financial consultant (ChFC), chartered life underwriter (CLU), accredited personal financial specialist (APFS) who are also CPAs.

Can I expect a financial planner to service all of my financial planning needs?

Financial planners are basically generalists, and might not have expertise in all areas relevant to financial planning such as estate and retirement plans, investments, insurance, and planning for the education of children. In devising an appropriate financial plan, a planner often consults with other professionals such as lawyers, insurance agents, and stockbrokers. In this way, a financial planner supplements his or her knowledge with the expertise of other qualified professionals.

How long does it take to prepare a financial plan, and what does the plan include?

A formal financial plan may take from one to three months to prepare, depending on the number of areas covered. It generally includes a profile of your current net worth, an analysis projecting future income, and the planner's recommendations.

Is there any protection for accounts with a stockbrokerage?

The Securities Investor Protection Corporation (SIPC) provides a form of insurance for clients of brokerage firms that fail or are forced into bankruptcy. Limits of protection are $500,000 per customer, while claims for cash are limited to $100,000 per customer.

What is the difference between a full-service broker and a discount broker?

The basic difference relates to the extent of service provided by each type of broker. In addition to buying and selling securities on behalf of a customer, a full-service broker also provides investment ideas and professional guidance on buy and sell decisions. A discount broker restricts duties to executing buy and sell decisions initiated by a customer.

How should I monitor my account with a stockbroker?

Carefully review the account statements mailed to you by the brokerage firm, which may be monthly or quarterly. Review all the activity noted on the statement, such as dividends and buy and sell transactions. Question any activity that you do not recognize. Also, ask the broker to provide you with current research reports on companies in which you invest.

I suspect there is a problem with my account that cannot be resolved with the branch manager or broker at my brokerage firm, what other recourse do I have?

There are several agencies that can mediate disputes between customer and stockbroker. You can file a formal written complaint to any of the following: Securities and Exchange Commission (SEC), National Association of Securities Dealers (NASD), Municipal Securities Rulemaking Board (MSRB), New York Stock Exchange (NYSE), or American Stock Exchange (AMEX).

When should I consider using a money manager?

A money manager should be engaged when you have at least

$100,000 to invest, lack sufficient time to make investment decisions, and are willing to keep your money invested over a prolonged time period (e.g., at least five years) despite volatility in the stock market.

How is a money manager different from a financial planner?

The range of services differs among these professionals. A money manager engages exclusively in portfolio management. A financial planner provides a variety of advisory services to a client, which may be based on general and/or specialized expertise and knowledge in matters relating to insurance, estate and retirement planning, and other areas. A money manager is usually given discretionary power over investment transactions without client approval. A financial planner consults with a client before engaging in any transaction.

If I cannot find a money manager through referrals from friends and business associates, what's the next-best approach?

Consider using an independent management consultant, often referred to as a "talent scout," who will track the performance records of money managers for a fee, and then match you with a compatible money manager. These individuals often work as financial planners and charge high fees (e.g., $1,500 or more). For an additional fee, an independent management consultant will also monitor the performance of your money manager with respect to managing your portfolio and will advise you as to whether or not the money manager should be retained.

When discussing fees for a CPA's services, what should specifically cover with the CPA?

Inquire as to the following: benefits to be received from the services, estimated hours to complete the engagements, the hourly or daily rate to be charged, estimated out-of-pocket expenses (e.g., travel, lodging), and method of billing (e.g. monthly, quarterly).

If I have a justifiable complaint against a CPA for any wrongdoing or what appears to be an unethical business practice, what matter of recourse do I have?

You may register a complaint with the Professional Ethics Division of the American Institute of Certified Public Accountants (AICPA). The AICPA administers and interprets the Code of Professional Conduct to be followed by CPAs who are AICPA members and can discipline a CPA if a complaint is found to be justifiable.

How do financial planners charge for their services?

Financial planners charge for their services based on an hourly fee, commission, or a combination of both fee and commission. A "fee only" planner may charge an hourly fee, a flat fee, or a percentage fee based on your net worth. Some financial planners charge a commission on the investment products they sell, which might be eight percent on a mutual fund investment, for example. On the other hand, other planners may work out a fee arrangement that combines a final dollar amount or fee and a commission on the investment product sold.

Is it necessary to have an engagement letter from a financial planner?

You should request an engagement letter from the financial planner that covers the services to be provided and the objectives of the financial plan. In this way, you ensure that your financial planning goals coincide with the plan, and avoid any misunderstandings and/or uncertainties between you and your planner.

If I believe that I've been misled by a financial planner with whom might I register a complaint?

Register your complaint with the Securities and Exchange Commission (SEC) if the planner is SEC-registered. Further, if your planner is a certified financial planner, register your complaint with the International Board of Standards and Practices for Certified Financial Planners (IBCFP), which is an organization that oversees the certification of CFPs.

How can I check on the background of a stockbroker who I am considering to handle my account?

The National Association of Securities Dealers (NASD), the self-regulatory group for the over-the-counter (OTC) market, can provide you with a summary of the education, employment history, and any criminal or disciplinary record of NASD registered stockbrokers. This can be accomplished by submitting an "Information Request Form" on the stockbroker of your choice and sending it to the NASD. This form can be obtained by writing to the NASD Membership Department, P.O. Box 9401, Gaithersburg, Maryland 20898, or call the information services line at (301) 738-6500. State securities administrators can provide a similar background check on stockbrokers or the brokerage firms conducting business in the state. Your state administrator's telephone number can be obtained by calling the North American Securities Administrators Association at (800) 942-9022.

Are there investments other than stocks and bonds that a stockbrokerage firm can provide to its customers?

Most brokerage firms provide a broad array of retail services that includes many investment products. These products may include limited partnerships, index options and futures, life insurance and annuities, mortgage backed securities, mutual funds, and unit investment trusts to name a few. The larger brokerage firms all carry a long list of investment products to offer customers.

How much does a money manager or investment counselor charge for managing a portfolio?

Fee schedules may be based on sliding scale or a flat fee. A sliding scale fee is a certain percentage of total assets which is assessed annually and descends as the account size increases. For example, in the first year you might be charged two percent of total assets and one percent of total assets in future years if the total assets or value of the portfolio increases. On the other hand, a flat fee may be charged by a money manager or investment counselor which is usually set at a minimum amount regardless of the size of the account.

Are there any clues or warning signs that will reveal questionable handling of my account?

Clues or warning signs that indicate a troublesome investment counseling firm may include any one or all of the following items:

- Another manager is assigned to your portfolio.
- Key employees have left the firm.
- The firm has lost some major clients.
- Your portfolio's performance is below major indices, such as the S&P 500.
- The firm's ownership has changed hands.
- Personal attention to your account appears to be lacking, and/or telephone calls to your portfolio manager are not returned promptly.

How can I check the background and qualifications of a money manager?

Money managers are required to register with the Securities and Exchange Commission (SEC) as investment advisers, and must submit an ADV form to the SEC which includes certain information about the adviser such as: management fees or a description of the adviser's investment strategy, educational background and work experience. Ask the money manager for copies of parts one and two of the ADV form. The form also reveals whether the money manager has been the subject of an SEC lawsuit or any other problems.

APPENDIX A—INTERVIEW QUESTIONNAIRE

(Certified Public Accountant)

1. How long has the firm been in business?
2. What is the organizational structure of the firm (i.e., partners or shareholders, managers, staff accountants, number of offices)?
3. How many CPAs comprise the professional staff?
4. Are the CPAs in the firm members of the American Institute of CPAs (AICPA) and the state societies of CPAs within the state of the firm's practice?
5. Has the firm participated in a practice-monitoring program, such as the peer-review program of the AICPA Division for CPA Firms, or the quality-review program? If so, what were the results?
6. Is the firm a member of any professional association of CPAs other than the AICPA?
7. What is the nature and extent of services provided by the firm to clients?
8. What types of clients does the firm service (i.e., individuals, closely held companies, publicly held companies, etc.)?
9. Does the firm specialize in any particular industries?
10. Does the firm provide a continuing professional education (CPE) program for each of its professional staff?
11. What is the nature and extent of the firm's involvement in practice-development activities?
12. How does the firm arrive at its fees?
13. Does the firm maintain adequate liability insurance?
14. Are there any pending legal suits against the firm?
15. Can the firm's clients be used as reference checks?

APPENDIX B—INTERVIEW QUESTIONNAIRE

(Financial Planner)

1. What is the extent of your formal education (college, graduate degree, areas of study)?
2. What are your financial planning credentials?
   - Certified financial planner (CFP)?
   - Chartered financial consultant (ChFC)?
   - Chartered life underwriter (CLU)?
   - Registry of Financial Planning Practitioners?
   - Accredited personal financial specialist (APFS)?
3. What was your profession prior to becoming a financial planner (accountant, lawyer, insurance agent, stockbroker, etc.)?
4. How long have you been providing financial planning services?
5. What are your areas of specialization?
6. Are you registered as an investment adviser with the SEC?
7. How large is your firm (number of personnel and offices)?
8. How many clients do you represent? Are they individuals and/or businesses?
9. Are you a member of any professional financial planning associations?
   - Institute of Certified Financial Planners (ICFP)?
   - International Association for Financial Planning (IAFP)?
   - Registry of Financial Planning Practitioners?
   - National Association of Personal Financial Advisers (NAPFA)?
10. Do you take continuing professional education (CPE) in financial planning each year?

11. Have you ever been cited by a professional or regulatory group for disciplinary actions?
12. Is your firm registered with your state securities office?
13. How are you compensated for services (fee only, commissions only, fees and commissions)?
14. Will you, or one of your associates, prepare my financial plan?
15. Will you consult with other professionals (e.g., lawyers, insurance agents) during the preparation of my financial plan?
16. Does the service include recommendations for specific investments or investment products?
17. Will you be involved with the implementation of my financial plan?
18. Can you provide me with continual advice whenever my financial situation changes?
19. Can you provide me with some sample financial plans that were prepared for your clients whose objectives and goals were similar to mine?
20. Can you provide me with the names of three clients with situations similar to mine that you have served during the past three years?

APPENDIX C—INTERVIEW QUESTIONNAIRE

(Money Manager)

1. What is the minimum account size your firm will handle?
2. What are the backgrounds and qualifications of the portfolio managers in your firm?
3. Is there a limit to the number of accounts a portfolio manager will manage?
4. What is your fee structure and how is it determined?
5. How often will my portfolio manager review my account (e.g., daily, weekly)?
6. How often will we meet to discuss and review the performance of my portfolio?
7. Based on your experience, what form of investment approach seems to work the best (i.e., investment style and philosophy)?
8. What sources of research does your firm use in managing portfolios?
9. What has been the firm's annual rate of return for the past five years?
10. Are management fees and trading costs deducted from the expected return on investment?

APPENDIX D—INTERVIEW QUESTIONNAIRE

(Stockbroker)

1. Is your firm a member of the following:
   - A recognized stock exchange, such as the New York Stock Exchange (NYSE) or the American Stock Exchange (AMEX)?
   - The National Association of Securities Dealers (NASD)?
   - The Securities Investors Protection Corporation (SIPC)?
2. What kinds of investment products does your firm provide?
3. Does the firm provide different investment options (e.g., margin accounts, discretionary accounts)?
4. What is the extent of your experience in the securities industry?
5. Based on your experience, have you determined whether any one investment product works best for your clients?
6. What size portfolios do you manage?
7. What kinds of information does your firm's research department have available to clients (e.g., annual reports, prospectuses)?
8. Do members of your firm give seminars on investing topics?
9. How are your fees determined and what are the factors used in making that determination?
10. Have there been any complaints against your firm regarding questionable trading practices?
11. What industries do you foresee as possessing the most productive future potential in the stock market?
12. As a client, what kind of service can I expect from you? (This includes the following: 1) recommendations on investment opportunities, including relevant research

data, 2) periodic calls on the current status of investment holdings, along with recommendations as to when to sell certain investments, and 3) semiannual and/or annual reviews of investment portfolio).

13. Can you provide me with names and addresses of some of your clients as reference checks?

14. Is your firm a member of any trade association, such as the Securities Industry Association (SIA)?

15. Do you have any suggestions as to how I might evaluate your performance when it comes to investment recommendations?

GLOSSARY

Accounting services various forms of services performed by certified public accountants (CPAs) that relate to the maintenance of accounting records.

Accredited Personal Financial Specialist (APFS) a title awarded by the American Institute of Certified Public Accountants (AICPA) to CPAs who meet certain education and experience requirements in providing financial planning services to clients.

ADV form a form required to be filed by investment advisers with the Securities and Exchange Commission (SEC) that describes certain information relating to the investment adviser's background, education, and work experience.

American College an educational institution that offers a curriculum in financial planning leading to a designation as a Chartered Financial Consultant (ChFC) and/or a Chartered Life Underwriter (CLU).

American Institute of Certified Public Accountants (AICPA) the largest national professional organization of certified public accountants (CPAs).

American Society of CLU & ChFC a trade association of financial planners, members of which must be a Chartered Life Underwriter (CLU) or a Chartered Financial Consultant (ChFC).

American Stock Exchange (AMEX) the second largest stock exchange in the United States.

Annual report a common report issued by publicly listed companies to its shareholders and other interested parties that contains financial information and other relevant data on a company's products and/or services.

Appellate division an appeal board of the Internal Revenue Service (IRS) where a taxpayer may appeal an IRS agent's decision on an audited income-tax return.

Arbitration a mechanism used to resolve any disputes between individuals and their stockbrokers.

Association for Investment Management and Research (AIMR) a professional association of money managers and investment counseling firms.

Audit an examination of financial statements by a certified public accountant (CPA).

Audit report a CPA's report on the results of an audit or examination of financial statements.

Balance sheet a financial statement that reports a company's assets, liabilities, and net worth (equity) at a specific point in time, usually at the end of the year.

Bear market a time when stocks and bonds continue to sink in value, or remain at low value.

Blue chip a term used to describe stocks of large and well-established companies, such as General Motors, IBM, and AT&T.

Boiler-room operation a questionable method of selling highly speculative or worthless securities by telephone.

Bull market a time when stocks and bonds continue to rise in value.

Certified Financial Planner (CFP) a title conferred to those who fulfill certain education and work experience requirements in financial planning.

Certified Public Accountant (CPA) a state-licensed professional accountant who has met certain statutory requirements regarding education, testing by examination, and employment.

Chartered Financial Analyst (CFA) a professional designation conferred on individuals who demonstrate competence in investment analysis through a series of examinations and investment-related work experience.

Chartered Financial Consultant (ChFC) a title conferred by the American College to those who complete an extensive study program in financial planning and possess related work experience.

Chartered Life Underwriter (CLU) a title conferred by the American College on those who complete an extensive study program in either life insurance planning or personal insurance planning, and who possess related work experience in the insurance industry.

Churning excessive trading in a customer's account by a stockbroker in order to earn commissions.

Code of ethics rules and standards of practice for financial planners to follow when servicing clients.

Code of professional conduct rules and related interpretations on ethical practices for Certified Public Accountants (CPAs) to follow when servicing clients.

College for Financial Planning an educational institution that offers a curriculum in financial planning that leads to a designation as a Certified Financial Planner (CFP).

Commodities futures representative a broker who is certified by the SEC to sell all types of commodities and futures.

Compilation a service performed by a Certified Public Accountant (CPA) that includes gathering or pulling together (i.e., compiling) information in a financial statement format.

Compilation report a CPA's report on a compilation of financial statements.

Continuing Professional Education (CPE) educational program taken by professionals, such as CPAs and financial planners, on an annual basis in order to reinforce and update their technical knowledge.

Discount broker a stockbroker whose services are generally restricted to buying and selling securities for clients.

Discretionary account an account with a stockbrokerage for which the broker has authority to initiate buy and sell orders without client approval.

Division for CPA Firms a self-regulatory program of the American Institute of Certified Public Accountants (AICPA). Public accounting firms must meet certain AICPA membership requirements that ensure compliance with professional standards in accounting and auditing.

Dow Jones Industrial Average an index used to measure the stock market as a whole that comprises stocks of thirty blue-chip companies.

Engagement letter a form of written contract between a professional, such as a CPA or a financial planner, and a client that describes the nature and extent of services to be performed and the related fee.

Financial Accounting Standards Board (FASB) an organization that is responsible for establishing financial accounting and reporting standards for companies to follow in preparation of financial statements.

Financial plan a formal written document prepared by a financial planner for a client that is designed to help the client achieve certain financial objectives.

Financial statement a numerical or quantitative picture or representation of a company's or individual's financial position at a given point in time (e.g., year end).

Freedom of Information Act an act of Congress that allows public access to various forms of documented information, such as investigations and litigation relevant to stockbrokers.

Full-service broker a stockbroker who provides guidance on buy and sell decisions for securities transactions, and who executes such transactions.

General securities registered representative an SEC-licensed stockbroker.

Generally Accepted Accounting Principles (GAAP) accounting principles and practices that govern rules for financial accounting and reporting.

Generally Accepted Auditing Standards (GAAS) rules and criteria followed by Certified Public Accountants (CPAs) in the performance of audits.

Growth Stock Outlook a weekly newsletter that reports on stock-market activity and provides an analysis of individual stocks.

Income statement a financial statement that reports on a company's revenues and expenses for a period of time (e.g., one year).

Institute for Investment Consultants a professional association of management consultants who track the performance of money managers for a fee.

Institute of Certified Financial Planners (ICFP) a trade association of financial planners.

Internal control structure the methods and procedures used by a company for ensuring protection of assets and reliability of financial records.

Internal Revenue Service (IRS) a federal government agency responsible for developing rules and regulations concerning taxation matters.

International Association of Financial Planning (IAFP) a worldwide nonprofit professional trade association for financial planners.

International Board of Standards and Practices for Certified Financial Planners (IBCFP) an independent, non-profit organization that oversees the administration of the Certified Financial Planner (CFP) comprehensive certification process.

Investment Advisers Act of 1940 an act of Congress that requires investment advisers who provide investment advice for compensation to be registered with the Securities and Exchange Commission (SEC).

Investment company/variable contracts representative an SEC-registered broker who specializes in the sale of mutual funds, variable annuities, and profit-sharing and tax-annuity plans.

Investment Council Association of America (ICAA) a professional association of investment counseling firms.

Investment counseling firm a firm that specializes in portfolio management of stocks, bonds, and other securities.

Investment management consultant a financial planner who selects and monitors the performance of money managers for a fee.

Investment packages investment products sold by brokerage firms to clients. They include limited partnerships, index options and futures, life insurance and annuities, mortgage-backed securities, and unit investment trusts.

Kiplinger's *Personal Finance* magazine a monthly magazine that reports on business activity, including the stock market.

Management Advisory Services (MAS) management consulting services provided by Certified Public Accountants (CPAs) relating to areas such as implementing information systems, special studies on asset management and cost reduction, and organizational structure.

Margin account an account with a stockbrokerage in which the firm loans a client a part of the price for the securities purchased and the securities are held as collateral by the firm.

Market Logic a weekly newsletter that reports on stock market activity and provides an analysis of individual stocks.

Money **magazine** a monthly magazine that reports on business activities, including the stock market.

Money manager an investment adviser who is responsible

for managing a client's portfolio, and for buying and selling securities on behalf of the client.

Municipal Securities Rulemaking Board (MSRB) an agency that regulates the underwriting, trading, and selling of municipal securities.

National Association of Personal Financial Advisers the largest nationwide organization of fee-only financial planners.

National Association of Securities Dealers (NASD) the association that supervises the trading of over-the-counter stocks by member brokers and dealers of securities.

New York Stock Exchange (NYSE) the largest stock exchange in the United States.

North American Securities Administrators Association (NASAA) a trade association that provides background checks on stockbrokers within states.

Notes to Financial Statements (or footnotes) narrative information included with financial statements that is designed to clarify and explain the significance of items addressed in the financial statements.

Over-the-counter (OTC) a stock-market term that refers to securities bought and sold through brokers, but not on the floor of a stock exchange. OTC trades usually involve stocks of small companies.

Peer Review a practice-monitoring program of the AICPA Division for CPA Firms that encompasses a review by Certified Public Accountants of other CPA or public accounting firms' quality-control system as it relates to accounting and auditing practices.

Personal financial planning a means of developing a comprehensive and integrated financial plan based on potential earnings, returns on investments, accumulated assets, and living expenses, in order to enable one to meet certain financial objectives.

Personal financial planning division a Division of the American Institute of Certified Public Accountants that is responsible for programs and standards relating to CPAs who are designated as Accredited Personal Financial Specialists (APFS).

Portfolio management a service provided by money managers and investment-counseling firms who buy and sell securities (i.e., a portfolio) on behalf of their clients.

Practice development a form of public relations engaged in by CPA or public accounting firms to enhance their professional image.

Private Companies Practice Section (PCPS) a section of the AICPA Division for CPA Firms that is reserved for public accounting firms serving privately held companies.

Professional Achievement in Continuing Education (PACE) a continuing-education program sponsored by the American College. The program is for financial planners with the designation Chartered Financial Consultant (ChFC) or Chartered Life Underwriter (CLU).

Professional Conduct Questionnaire a questionnaire filed annually by money managers with the Association for Investment Management and Research (AIMR) as a condition for membership.

Professional ethics division a division of the American Institute of CPAs that interprets and monitors the AICPA Code of Professional Conduct.

Public accounting a practice engaged in by certified public accountants to service clients in areas relating to accounting services, financial statements, taxation, and management advisory services.

Publicly held companies corporations that have their securities traded on a recognized stock exchange and are required to file financial statements with the Securities and Exchange Commission (SEC).

Quality-control system a form of checks and balances or internal control over a public accounting firm's accounting and auditing practices.

Quality review a practice-monitoring program of the American Institute of CPAs that is designed for CPA or public accounting firms with ten or fewer professionals, and focuses on the quality of the accounting and auditing practices of those firms.

The Registry of Financial Planning Practitioners (RFPP) a program sponsored by the International Association for Financial Planners (IAFP) that is designed to promote professional excellence in financial planning.

Review a service performed by a CPA to determine whether any significant matters affect a financial statement.

Review report a CPA's report on a review of financial statements.

SEC Practice Section (SECPS) a section of the AICPA Division for CPA Firms that is designed for public accounting firms that service publicly held companies.

Securities and Exchange Commission (SEC) an independent federal government agency that protects investors against abuse in the securities and financial markets, and oversees and regulates the securities industry.

Securities Industry Association (SIA) a trade association for brokerage firms.

Securities Investor Protection Corporation (SIPC) a nonprofit corporation created by Congress to protect clients of stockbrokerages that fail or are forced into bankruptcy.

Series 3 an examination, the passing of which leads to SEC certification as a commodity futures representative.

Series 6 an examination, the passing of which leads to SEC certification as an investment company/variable contracts representative.

Series 7 an examination, the passing of which leads to SEC certification as a general securities registered representative.

SROs self-regulatory organizations that monitor the securities industry, such as the Securities and Exchange Commission (SEC), and the National Association of Securities Dealers (NASD).

Standard & Poor's 500 (S&P 500) an index of the stock market as a whole that is based on the prices of 500 widely held stocks.

Standards of practice for member firms principles of conduct or code of ethics for investment counseling firms that are members of the Investment Council Association of America (ICAA).

Standards of professional conduct a code of ethics for money managers who are members of the Association for Investment Management and Research (AIMR).

State Boards of Accountancy organizations within each state or territory of the U.S. that are responsible for licensing Certified Public Accountants (CPAs).

Statement of cash flows a financial statement that reports a company's cash inflows and outflows.

Statement of changes in net worth a personal financial statement that presents changes in the net worth of an individual or family over a period of time (e.g., one year).

Statement of financial condition a personal financial statement that provides information on an individual's or family's net worth on a given date.

Statement of retained earnings (net worth) a financial statement that reconciles the retained earnings or net worth of a company from the beginning to the end of the year.

State Societies of CPAs organizations of Certified Public Accountants formed within a state to monitor and promote professionalism among its members.

Stockbrokers individuals who act as agents for buyers and sellers of securities.

Stock exchange a marketplace where stocks, bonds, and other investment securities are bought and sold.

Street name a term indicating that a stock certificate is held in possession by a brokerage firm on behalf of the shareholder.

Taxation services tax-related services provided by Certified Public Accountants, including income-tax-return preparation, consultation on tax matters, determining compliance with tax law, and representation before taxation authorities.

Trade a term used to describe the matching of a bid and offer price for a security when it is bought and sold on a recognized stock exchange.

Value Line Investment Survey a weekly newsletter that reports on stock-market activity and provides an analysis of individual stocks.

Wall Street Journal a daily newspaper that reports on economic and business activity, including the stock market.

Wrap fee a fee arrangement with an investment counseling firm that provides a variety of investment-related services.

INDEX

More selected BARRON'S titles:

DICTIONARY OF ACCOUNTING TERMS
Siegel and Shim
Nearly 2500 terms related to accounting are defined.
Paperback, $10.95, Can. $14.50 (3766-9)

DICTIONARY OF ADVERTISING AND DIRECT MAIL TERMS
Imber and Toffler
Nearly 3000 terms used in the ad industry are defined.
Paperback, $10.95, Can. $14.50 (3765-0)

DICTIONARY OF BANKING TERMS
Fitch
Nearly 3000 terms related to banking, finance and money
management.
Paperback, $10.95, Can. $14.50 (3946-7)

DICTIONARY OF BUSINESS TERMS
Friedman, general editor
Over 6000 entries define business terms.
Paperback, $10.95, Canada $14.50 (3775-8)

BARRON'S BUSINESS REVIEW SERIES
These guides explain topics covered in a college-level business
course.
Each book: paperback
ACCOUNTING, 2nd EDITION. *Eisen.* $11.95, Can. $15.95 (4375-8)
BUSINESS LAW, *Hardwicke and Emerson.* $11.95, Can. $15.95 (3495-3)
BUSINESS STATISTICS, *Downing and Clark.* $11.95, Can. $15.95 (3576-3)
ECONOMICS, *Wessels.* $11.95, Can. $15.50 (3560-7)
FINANCE, 2nd EDITION. *Groppelli and Nikbakht.* $11.95,
Can. $15.95 (4373-1)
MANAGEMENT, *Montana and Charnov.* $11.95, Can. $15.50 (3559-3)
MARKETING, *Sandhusen.* $11.95, Can. $15.95 (3494-5)
QUANTITATIVE METHODS, *Downing and Clark.* $10.95,
Can. $14.95 (3947-5)

TALKING BUSINESS SERIES: BILINGUAL DICTIONARIES
Five bilingual dictionaries translate about 3000 terms not found in
most foreign phrasebooks.
Each book: paperback
TALKING BUSINESS IN FRENCH, *Le Gal.* $9.95, Can. $13.95
(3745-6)
TALKING BUSINESS IN GERMAN, *Strutz.* $9.95, Can. $12.95
(3747-2)
TALKING BUSINESS IN ITALIAN, *Rakus.* $8.95, Can. $11.95
(3754-5)
TALKING BUSINESS IN JAPANESE, *C. Akiyama and N. Akiyama.*
$9.95, Can. $12.95 (3848-7)
TALKING BUSINESS IN KOREAN, *Cheong.* $8.95, Can. $11.95
(3992-0)
TALKING BUSINESS IN SPANISH, *Fryer and Faria.* $9.95,
Can. $13.95 (3769-3)

All prices are in U.S. and Canadian dollars and subject to change without notice.
At your bookseller, or order direct adding 10% postage (minimum charge $1.75,
Canada $2.00), N.Y. residents add sales tax. ISBN PREFIX: 0-8120

Barron's Educational Series, Inc.
250 Wireless Boulevard, Hauppauge, NY 11788
Call toll-free: 1-800-645-3476
In Canada: Georgetown Book Warehouse
34 Armstrong Ave., Georgetown, Ontario L7G 4R9
Call toll-free: 1-800-247-7160

TITLES THAT GENERATE SUCCESS!

Business Success Series

Eight titles introduce Barron's new and innovative series designed to help the business person succeed 8 ways! Seasoned professionals offer common sense advice and facts on how to master job techniques that will generate success. Also included are interesting and informative case histories and insightful quotes. Each book: Paperback, $4.95, Can. $6.50, 96 pp., 4 3/16" x 7"

Conduct Better Job Interviews Wilson (4580-7)
Making Presentations With Confidence Buchan (4588-2)
Winning With Difficult People Bell & Smith (4583-1)
How To Negotiate a Bigger Raise Hartman (4604-8)
Running a Meeting That Works Miller (4640-4)
Time Management Hochheiser (4792-3)
Using the Telephone More Effectively Bodin (4672-2)
Motivating People Smith (4673-0)
Writing Effective Letters and Memos Bell (4674-9)

Prices subject to change without notice. Books may be purchased at your bookstore or by mail from Barron's. Enclose check or money order for total amount plus sales tax where applicable and 10% for postage and handling (minimum charge of $1.75 Canada $2.00). ISBN PREFIX: 0-8120

Barron's Educational Series, Inc.
250 Wireless Blvd., Hauppauge, NY 11788
In Canada: Georgetown Book Warehouse
34 Armstrong Ave., Georgetown, Ont. L7G 4R9